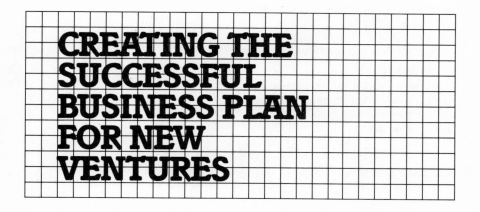

CREATING THE SUCCESSFUL BUSINESS PLAN FOR NEW VENTURES

LaRue Hosmer
Roger Guiles

McGraw-Hill Book Company

New York   St. Louis   San Francisco   Auckland   Bogotá   Hamburg
Johannesburg   London   Madrid   Mexico   Montreal   New Dehli
Panama   Paris   São Paulo   Singapore   Sydney   Toyko   Toronto

Library of Congress Cataloging in Publication Data

Hosmer, LaRue T.
    Creating the successful business plan for new ventures.

    Includes index.
    1.   New business enterprises—Planning.   2.   Small
business—Planning   I.   Guiles, Roger.   II.   Title.
HD62.5.H65   1985   658'.022   84-19472
ISBN 0-07-030452-1

1234567890   DOC/DOC   8987654

ISBN 0-07-030452-1

The editors for this book were Martha Jewett and Nancy Young, the designer was
Dennis Sharkey, and the production supervisor was Thomas G. Kowalczyk.
It was set in Garamond Light by Centennial Graphics.
Printed and bound by R.R. Donnelley and Sons Company.

CONTENTS

PREFACE

Nearly everyone at some time or another thinks, "I'd like to go into business for myself." Others who already have taken the first step say inwardly, "I'd like to turn my small company into a large corporation." If you have had one or the other of these thoughts lately, then this book is for you. Just take the principles of business planning given here, add a lot of hard work, and, with a little luck, you will succeed.

Starting a business or expanding a going enterprise requires answers to tough questions. Some are personal: "Is it worth it to me?" And others, practical: "Will the product appeal to the customer?" In this book we offer no help whatsoever in facing the personal questions; too many other how-to books never get past them. We believe the practical questions are most difficult to answer and most important to address.

Besides, if you cannot believe in your new venture, who will? We would not encourage you to start even a lemonade stand when plagued by self-doubt.

What we do encourage is development of creative entrepreneurial businesses—based on sound ideas, backed by careful planning, and supportive of the communities from which they arise. If you can accomplish all this, you will naturally acquire self-confidence and attract community help. Political officeholders and other economy-watchers have noticed that small businesses today are generating many new jobs and that big businesses continually add to the unemployment rolls. They will want your new venture to succeed because people like you now make the glue that holds our national economy together.

By all accounts the 1980s have unleashed an entrepreneurial boom. One in fourteen working adults is self-employed, or nearly eight million people in 1984, according to the U.S. Small Business Administration. And the rush to small business formation appears to be accelerating. In 1981, the last year for which information is available,

582,000 small businesses were formed, up 54 percent from 1976 and 102 percent from 1971.

If you have chosen to join the ranks of the self-employed or to cultivate a bigger market for your existing business, we applaud you and offer modest help. This book is designed to assist in the successful development of small and medium-sized companies with up to $30 million annual sales. It can lead you to avoid common mistakes of business formation, to chart a path of sustained company growth, and to know when you have reached your limit in any one product, service, or process field.

This book will not help you to take over the market by storm in a highly competitive industry; it suggests you should look elsewhere for a better opportunity. And it does not offer much consolation to business owners who want to stay small and private; our book presumes that you seek to build a high-growth company, perhaps eventually becoming a publicly held corporation.

As we advise new company founders to do, we have aimed our product, this book, at a particular audience. You fit our market profile if you have: (1) a strong urge to build your own organization, (2) a penchant for creative risk-taking, and (3) firsthand experience in a start-up business. These are the three most widely accepted characteristics of a budding entrepreneur. He or she resents control by others, revels in risk-taking, and, while looking over the shoulder of someone who has previously launched a business—perhaps a family member or an employer—thinks, "This is not so hard. I can do it better."

You should consider several different business fields before deciding exactly what you will attempt to do better. There are good ideas and bad, as you may learn from reading further. High levels of personal energy and perseverance will become equally important in your new venture. It takes one of each, a good entrepreneur and a good idea, to create the successful business plan.

We wish to thank several people and one institution for their help in producing this book. Melinda Grenier Guiles edited Chapter 1 after the two of us had nearly given up hope of reaching agreement. Deborah A. Rapley typed and retyped the manuscript during evenings and weekends. When we were concerned about meeting deadlines, her sister, Katheryn G. Helm, doubled the output. The University of Michigan provided an occasion for the two of us to meet and share ideas.

There, we have collaborated on an annual seminar, a business plan, and a book. We trust this is just the beginning of a productive, venturesome association.

LaRue Hosmer

Roger Guiles

CHAPTER ONE
THE BUSINESS PLAN

There are 14.5 million small businesses in the United States today, and the number steadily grows.

Each year approximately 1 million new ventures appear, and somewhat fewer existing companies disappear. Some of these vanishing small businesses are purchased by much larger corporations for their products or technologies. Others grow into medium-sized companies, often changing names and locations in the process. But the vast majority simply fail. It is generally believed that more than half of all new ventures fail in their first 2 years of operation and nearly 80 percent succumb within 5 years. Dying with them are the efforts, hopes, and investment dollars of their founders.

If you were to interview several of the casualties among small business owners, they probably would insist their unsuccessful efforts were due to lack of financing. "We didn't have enough money," they would say.

We believe, on the other hand, the cause of early business failures is more basic—and more easily solved. From our point of view, the problem is lack of planning. Company founders failed to define product features, identify market segments, recognize customer needs, prepare production methods, anticipate financial cash flows, and assign management tasks before starting. Consequently they ran out of money before the company became established. Careful, detailed planning is needed to form a successful new business.

THE HIGH-GROWTH FIRM

Effective planning is especially important for a new breed of small business: the high-growth firm. These are businesses that start small and expand exponentially by developing new products, serving new markets, or designing new processes that respond to immediate and growing needs in society. Such businesses are especially important today because our national economy is switching from capital-based industries such as steel, petrochemicals, and automobiles to knowl-edge-based industries such as telecommunications, data processing, and health care. Computers and automation are altering the way many companies operate, particularly in such business fields as financial services, distribution and transportation, and retail sales. Family life is also changing because of rapid growth in the number of working couples who may now enjoy greater income but less leisure. Environ-mental improvement, industrial redevelopment, and worker retraining are among today's important issues, receiving expanded public and private funding. All of these changes are creating fresh opportunities for new businesses—particularly small, flexible, creative firms.

Policymakers, by and large, have come to accept the notion that technological innovation and economic growth are stifled by industrial bigness. Massive companies, like ocean-going supertankers, operate efficiently only when proceeding straight ahead, carrying familiar cargo toward a predestined port. Small businesses are more adaptable and can respond to new opportunities by developing new products, mar-kets, or processes.

If there is any doubt in your mind about the truth of these assertions, notice what corporate America has been doing lately. Big companies are emulating small business by forming independent, specialized new-concept development teams. This approach has not been overly successful, however. The most revolutionary new ideas seems to be the province of small companies and individual entrepreneurs.

The potential for new products, markets, or processes developed by high-growth companies may be exceptionally large because demand is national or international, not local. A small business formed to sell automobiles or television sets, on the one hand, is limited in growth potential because it can serve customers only within a narrow geo-graphic territory and because it will encounter large numbers of established competitors. A small company formed to sell computer software or medical diagnostic devices, on the other hand, can serve customers across the country, even worldwide, and it may have no competitors at the start. Large market areas and lack of established competition mark the high-growth firm.

It is often thought that companies with high-growth potential are restricted to business fields which develop and use advanced technologies; microelectronics, genetic engineering, and industrial robotics certainly have received much media attention. But, medium- and low-technology products and services also may offer high-growth potential, particularly as they respond to expanding needs.

For example, companies formed to produce office furniture designed for use with computer keyboards, video screens, and printers have been quite successful. Yet their association with high technology is peripheral. Other medium- and low-technology products and services also can form the basis for high-growth firms including fast-food restaurants, indoor racket clubs, tax preparation services, personal financial consultants, wood stove manufacturers, and jogging equipment retailers.

Therefore, advanced technologies are not the key to starting high-growth firms. Company founders must analyze and understand the major changes taking place within society and possess the imagination to create a new product, a new market, or a new process which responds to one of these changes. The new product, market, or process can have a technological orientation—a better way of doing things—or a customer orientation—a better way of serving people. A better way, not a higher technology, is the basis for the formation of most successful high-growth firms.

THE NEED FOR PLANNING

Forming a small company based on a new product, market, or process is different from starting a small business based on preexisting products, markets, or processes. A new automobile repair shop or steel distribution warehouse, for example, can operate according to traditional practices and procedures. Proven management methodology may even come prepackaged as part of a franchise kit. Little planning

may be needed for such traditional ventures beyond routine projections of sales revenues and expenses.

A new repair service for medical electronics equipment or a distribution center for robotic components, on the other hand, probably
represent the first of their kind. Aspiring entrepreneurs in such nontra-
ditional industries must research market potential, develop a marketing
plan, design a production process, forecast financial needs, prepare
organizational systems, and anticipate problems of company growth.
Planning is central to the formation of these newer types of businesses.

To obtain capital and recruit people—both of which are needed to
make a new venture go—planning results must be summarized in a
single document, "the business plan." A carefully prepared business
plan is crucial to the success of a high-growth, high-potential company
because it helps convince others that your new idea, your special
insight, has genuine commercial merit. Persuading others may not be
easy if you are suggesting avenues never taken before. The business
plan explains your rationale and describes your chosen route to market entry.

THE NEW IDEA

Small companies start with a new idea. It may be a better way of doing
things based upon a different application of a fundamental technology,
or it may be a better way of serving customers based upon a different
understanding of a market need or a production method. Either way,
your idea—together with some money, a management team, and a lot
of faith—provides the reason for going into business.

One new idea is only a part of the total formation process, however.
This is what makes small business formation so interesting, so complex, and occasionally so frustrating. Many people believe a new concept plus a source of venture capital are the only requirements for
success, but much more is needed.

To become successful, your new business should include an entire
package of components. This package has to be complete, with logic
inherent in all its parts. These components may be gathered in any
sequence, but they all must exist, and they all should receive approximately equal priority. When one of these essential parts is either omit-

ted or neglected in the whole, that omission or neglect almost surely seems to lead directly toward business failure.

We believe there are seven elements of a successful formation package.

1. **Technical competence.** Someone within your formation team has to understand the relevant technology. This technology may concern solid-state physics or fast-food preparation, but your understanding must be on the level of intuitive mastery, not superficial acquaintance or constrained specialization. Technical problems of many kinds will crop up during the preformation planning, formal start-up, and early growth stages of a business. The venture is very vulnerable at these stages, and prompt, decisive resolution of problems is a necessity. Prompt, decisive resolution of technical problems comes only from a complete understanding of the technology at hand.

2. **Management skills.** Someone within the venture group has to understand the major business functions of marketing, production, and finance and the support services of cost accounting, data processing, and operational control. Your product concept—no matter how innovative—must be transformed into a marketable and producible good at a given cost and at a specific time. This transformation requires a range of management abilities. All of this expertise does not have to be fully developed among the formation team members, but it must be promptly available, when needed, from experienced professionals.

3. **Product (or service) concept.** The product concept *is* the new idea. Someone within the formation team has to have the technical imagination and the industry understanding necessary to envision a new product or service that fits a market need. This combination of industry understanding and technical imagination is central to product innovation in small companies. To gain momentum in early growth stages, it is best to conceive of a good or service that has not previously existed, but for which an immediate market demand does exist. Product innovation can result from individual activity or as an outcome of a group process. It provides a reason for success at the start.

4. **Financial resources.** The formation process can be divided into three distinct phases: a. "detailed planning" as the product concept

is transformed into a proven prototype, b. "formal start-up" as the prototype is offered for sale, and c. "early growth" as the sales begin to multiply. When it first became available, venture capital normally was offered to firms only in the third stage because venture capitalists required some confirmation that a market existed before investment. Recently, the typical injection of equity financing has moved back to the second stage and, in a few instances, to the first stage. In these early stages, invested capital has helped to intensify the interactive processes of product development and market research, which bring a product concept to a proven prototype. This is an encouraging development for potential entrepreneurs.

5. **Physical assets.** Working space and processing equipment are needed to convert the product concept to a proven prototype and then to begin production of the prototype. Traditionally, such physical assets have been considered a subset of start-up financing because of the reasonable expectation that with adequate money it is always possible to rent a building and buy machinery. It is more realistic to separate physical assets and financial resources. Simple space and standard equipment can be provided almost without risk. Property is reusable, but expenses for product development and market testing are not recoverable in the event of failure. Communities and other organizations are starting to provide these reusable assets at very low costs. This is another encouraging development for potential entrepreneurs.

6. **Business plan.** Starting a successful high-growth company is a risky, uncertain venture. The business plan provides a detailed and orderly study of these risks and uncertainties. It includes an examination of the proposed product (what are the advantages), the market (who are the customers), the industry (where are the competitors), the marketing policies (price, distribution, and promotion), the production methods (processes and costs), and the financial needs (working capital and fixed assets). The business plan schedules the activities necessary to bring a venture from product concept to early growth. It sets a completion time and estimated cost for each activity. The business plan says, "Here are the opportunities and problems we foresee, and this is what we expect to do about them."

7. **Personal drive.** Starting a successful high-growth company is often a slow and arduous task. The technical, managerial, conceptual,

physical, and financial components of the formation package have to be assembled, balanced, and combined. The business plan helps with some of this; it provides a verbal and numerical description of the needed activities. Yet somebody must want to see it happen and have the self-confidence to actively direct the others, particularly when things go wrong. This commitment is expressed as a personal drive to succeed for the sake of the product concept, not just for the individual. Such a committed individual says, "Here are the opportunities and problems we did not foresee, and this is what we are going to do about them."

Technical competence, management skills, a product concept, physical assets, financial resources, a business plan, and personal drive are the seven components needed to form a successful high-growth package. All are necessary. They must balance one another and interlock. In a sense, however, two are more critical than the others: the product concept and personal drive. All of the other components can be supplied by sources outside the venture group. Technical competence, management skills, physical assets, help with a business plan, and financial resources can be hired, rented, or purchased for money. You cannot hire, rent, or purchase a new idea or personal commitment.

Fortunately, personal commitment often seems to go hand in hand with a new product concept. People tend to become convinced of the worth of their own ideas. This combination of new ideas and personal drive, or of innovation and commitment, is our definition of an entrepreneur. You must have one or more such persons to start a high-growth company; the entrepreneur makes the small business formation process work.

Personal drive, we believe, represents some combination of self-confidence and energy level. There have been numerous studies of the personality characteristics of the entrepreneur. So far as we are aware, no definite conclusions have been reached.

Entrepreneurs, according to many studies, appear to be people with a high need for personal achievement and a low tolerance for organizational constraints. Unfortunately, these characteristics also may be used to describe baseball players, classical musicians, physical scientists, and many of the rest of us at one time or another in our lives. Since we cannot precisely define the personality traits of such an individual, perhaps the other quality of entrepreneurship should be considered: the new idea. What new ideas are suitable for small business formation? Where do they come from?

TYPES OF NEW IDEAS

New ideas suitable for starting small, high-growth companies tend not to be completely new products, designed for absolutely new markets, and produced by totally new processes. Small companies with limited technical, managerial, physical, and financial resources simply cannot afford to finance product-market-process breakthroughs of this nature. Such triple breakthroughs do occur. They are exciting when they happen, but they usually result in new industries rather than new companies. The development of semiconductor materials and the invention of genetic engineering methods are examples of triple breakthroughs leading to the formation of new industries.

Ideas for starting small, high-growth companies more often seem to be modifications of existing products, markets, and processes. They also appear to add one or, at most, two new elements to the product-market-process mix.

New high-growth firms may be based upon a new product for an existing market (as in the use of word processors for office equipment) or an existing product for a new market (as in the use of video tubes for arcade games) or a new process for an existing product and market (as in the use of fiber-reinforced plastics for automotive brake cylinders). There are a number of plausible combinations for such changes. The possible permutations are shown graphically in Figure 1-1.

SOURCES OF NEW IDEAS

Once you accept the notion that new ideas suitable for small business formation tend to be combinations of relatively minor changes or modifications in the product-market-process mix, the next questions are: Where do these ideas come from? How are they developed?

FIGURE 1-1 Graphic representation of possible product, market, and process combinations.

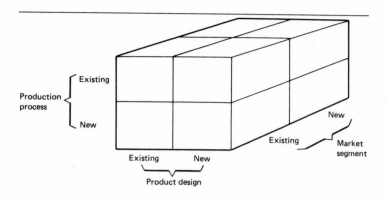

New ideas appear to come about as a result of someone observing a gap in a product line that needs filling, finding a niche in a market segment that can be better serviced, or discovering an opportunity to improve a production process. It is not at all clear how this recognition comes about or what provides the "spark." There seem to be two major avenues leading to product, market, or process recognition and, consequently, to the development of a new concept suitable for small business formation.

PRIOR EMPLOYMENT

Ideas for most technologically oriented products, markets, or processes apparently come from the founder's prior employment experiences. Arnold Cooper of Purdue University, while on a visiting appointment at Stanford, prepared a detailed and scholarly study of the formation of successful high-growth firms within the area.[1] He found that over 85 percent of Silicon Valley companies produced a product "substantially similar" to that manufactured by the prior employers of the founders and that these products used the "same general technol-

---

[1] Arnold C. Cooper, *The Founding of Technologically-Based Firms*, Center for Venture Management, Milwaukee, 1971.

ogy" or were sold to the "same general markets." These findings have been confirmed by numerous later studies.[2]

Prior employment experience as the source of new product concepts does make sense. The existing company provides industry understanding, joined with technical competence and management skills. All that is lacking is sufficient technological imagination to develop a product, market, or process concept. Technological imagination—the ability to envisage what is technically feasible—is not a common personal characteristic. But the existing company continually generates information about the other half of the innovative concept: What is commercially viable? It is not surprising that a union of the two halves so often does occur. The resulting progeny are called "spin-off" companies.

Prior employment as the source of new concepts helps to explain the "clustering" of high-growth companies in a limited number of geographic locations. The Bay Area south of San Francisco, Route 128 surrounding Boston, the Research Triangle in North Carolina, and Orange County in southern California are well-known examples of such concentrations. They come about because of the role of current employers in helping to generate product-market-process concepts and because of the historical models of earlier spin-offs which demonstrate that it is possible to start high-growth firms. The success of additional new firms, in turn, helps to attract an increased supply of needed physical assets and financial resources to the area. One new business success feeds on another.

Prior employment as the source of new product-market-process concepts creates both legal and ethical problems. The legal issues are complex and complicated by employment contracts, trade secrets, customer lists, and noncompetitive agreements. Courts in the areas of high-growth-company concentration tend to be clogged with suits and counter-suits addressing these issues. The ethical problems are no more easily resolved, though they may be expressed in simpler terms: What does a person owe his or her employer?

The legal and ethical issues surrounding prior employment as a source of product concepts for new business formation certainly can-

---

[2] See Arnold C. Cooper and John Komives, *Technical Entrepreneurship: A Symposium*, Center for Venture Management, Milwaukee, 1972, or Karl H. Vesper, *New Venture Strategies*, Prentice-Hall, Englewood Cliffs, N.J., 1980, for descriptions of other studies.

not be settled here. Legal questions will be decided in the courts; many ethical problems may be more apparent than real. Often, the prior employer rejects the new concept because it does not fit corporate strategy.

Two examples are legendary. Eugene Amdahl, founder of Amdahl Computer Corp., first offered his design of very large and fast machines to IBM, at which he was vice president of research. He was told that his design used components that were different from the balance of the company's product line. Thus, it would destroy manufacturing efficiencies and economies of scale. W. J. Saunders, the eventual founder of Advanced Micro Devices, asked Fairchild Camera and Instrument, at which he was vice president of marketing, to expand the sales of their integrated circuits from computer hardware to communication systems. He was told that this would increase selling costs. Many new firms are founded on rejected concepts, not pirated ideas.

PERSONAL EXPERIENCE

Product, market, or process concepts for most new technologically oriented companies come from prior employment, but many people do not work for high-technology firms. These individuals must rely on personal experiences as the basis for their observations and ideas. Many companies founded on the basis of such new ideas appear to have a customer orientation rather than a technological orientation. Yet, they often are equally successful.

Thomas Monaghan, founder of Domino's Pizza, began with a single store near a state university. He knew that college students liked pizza, and he was certain that making a standard 12-inch pizza would be faster and less expensive than making a wide variety of sizes. The Domino's Pizza chain now has over 2000 stores nationwide and is expanding internationally.

An Wang, founder of the company bearing his name, developed a computer terminal for decentralized data processing in 1955 based on the personal observation that many people disliked working with the usual punched-card input and line-printer output of centralized computer systems. Wang Laboratories Inc. sales now exceed $1.0 billion annually. Perhaps this company grew so rapidly because it began with both customer and technical orientations.

Starting a new company based upon personal experience rather than prior employment avoids many legal and ethical problems. But there can be personal problems. It is easy to mislead yourself, to think, "I like pizza; therefore everyone likes pizza" or "I don't like punch cards and batch processing; therefore everyone will prefer an on-line terminal." Investigation of a new concept based upon personal experience must be especially thorough to confirm the viability of the product and the existence of the market and to overcome personal biases and misconceptions.

THE BUSINESS PLAN

Now, you have a new idea (wherever it came from) and the personal drive to start a high-growth company. Where do you get everything else you need? From a business plan, a tool for raising the other components of the business formation package: the people and the money. The business plan also helps you determine if your idea is worth the effort and commitment needed to organize a start-up venture.

The business plan investigates in detail the feasibility of your proposal to extend a product line, serve a market segment, or improve a production process. It will involve a lot of hard work, and it will certainly test your level of personal drive. Yet, when your business plan is completed, you will no longer have to accept on faith the commercial viability of your idea. Neither will anyone else. Besides convincing yourself and others that your new concept is sound, the business plan creates a road map of activities needed to manage your growing firm, finance company operations, produce the product or service, market it, and maintain a competitive edge. In other words, the business plan takes an untried idea and, through the application of personal drive and hard work, translates it into reality. The business plan does all this by answering seven questions.

1. **Do you have a complete formation package?** You will need technical competence, management skills, a new idea, physical assets, financial resources, a business plan, and personal drive. Of these components, the new idea and the personal drive are the most

critical; with them, you can put together a business plan that will help you to gather the other components.

2. **Do you have a reason for success at the start and a competitive advantage over the long run?** Your new idea has to fill an immediate market need and be able to achieve a customer- or cost-advantage for continued success. Otherwise, existing firms may simply copy your idea and push you aside. (See Chapter 2, "Industry Analysis.")

3. **Can your product or service be marketed?** You must be able to make potential customers aware of your product or service by promotional means, offer it at a price they are willing to pay, and have it easily obtainable through distribution channels. Introduction of a new product or service which is either invisible, unaffordable, or unavailable is an invitation to disaster. (See Chapter 3, "Market Planning.")

4. **Can your product or service be manufactured?** To translate an idea into reality, you must be able to produce your product or service in adequate quantity to meet demand while achieving desirable cost and quality levels. Some of the most imaginative new product, market, or process concepts turn out to be technically impossible under conditions of actual production. You should discover such disappointing facts before starting your company, not afterward. (See Chapter 4, "Production Planning.")

5. **Can the marketing and manufacturing of your product or service be financed?** Nearly all new companies need money for fixed assets and working capital. You must analyze your current financial position, project your future needs, and then persuade others to risk their funds on your start-up venture. Common sources of needed capital are personal savings, commercial bank loans, and venture capital investments. (See Chapter 5, "Financial Planning.")

6. **Can your company's activities in marketing, manufacturing, and finance be managed?** Competent people must be selected for important functional and technical tasks; the actions and decisions of these people have to be coordinated for truly effective company operation. Competent people who work well together and demonstrate commitment can overcome inevitable problems of start-up venture operations. (See Chapter 6, "Organizational Planning.")

7. **Can you write a business plan which will be easily understood and logically convincing?** You must persuade competent people to join your start-up venture and others to provide financial help. You do this by preparing clear, convincing written proposals. (See Appendix A, "The Completed Business Plan" and Chapter 7, "Presentation of Written Reports.")

Preparing a business plan is a lengthy, detailed, and difficult process. Do not take it lightly. The amount of effort you expend in the planning stage will reduce the number of problems you encounter later. Through effective formation planning, you will avoid problems, gain self-confidence, and attract needed resources.

Each of the formation planning steps must be accomplished in the sequence presented here, from industry analysis to preparation of marketing, production, financial, and organizational plans. Do not try to take short cuts. Each step produces information needed for the next. The most critical steps in the process, however, are the first two. You must have an idea for a new product, market, or process. This idea must provide: 1. a reason for success at the start and 2. a competitive advantage over the long run. A lack of one or the other can render the balance of the planning process meaningless.

Well done, formation planning leads to success for your new company; poorly done, it almost surely leads to failure. There are exceptions, of course, because luck always plays a role. But formation planning limits the role of chance, improves the odds of your company's high growth, and increases the personal rewards which become part and parcel of continuing business achievement.

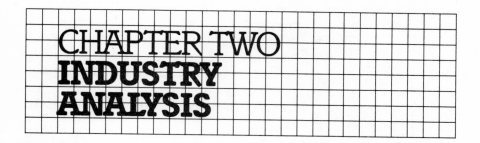

CHAPTER TWO
INDUSTRY
ANALYSIS

Formation planning begins with industry analysis. A new venture has to fit within an industry or create a new one. Few companies are able to create a new industry; this requires a quantum leap in technology and massive amounts of money. It is much easier to fit a company into an existing industry through product, market, or process innovation.

In the first chapter, we explained that most high-growth companies arise from a gap in a product line, a niche in a market segment, or an opportunity to improve a production process. This gap, niche, or opportunity provides the reason for success—something every new company should have at the start. Yet, more is needed to achieve profitability and growth over the long run. The new company must also develop a competitive advantage, a reason why a larger firm will not simply "make a copy" and push the smaller company out of the industry.

A reason for success at the start and a competitive advantage over the long run are both important. They help make it possible to recruit the people and raise the money needed for the venture. And they help reassure company founders that they have an idea worth pursuing.

An industry consists of a group of firms producing reasonably similar products for sale to reasonably similar customers by reasonably similar processes. Few companies start without competitors. You should acknowledge those competitors in your prospective industry and assess their positions within its structure. Then fit your new firm—with a distinctive product, market, or process concept—into that structure, avoiding direct competition at the start and developing a competitive advantage over the long run.

Avoidance of initial direct competition and later development of a competitive advantage require an understanding of industry structure.

This is why industry analysis is the starting point for formation planning. The new idea—about a gap in a product line, a niche in a market segment, or an opportunity in a production process—obviously comes first. But the essence of successful entrepreneurship lies in recognizing the potential of a new concept. No book can help you do that. But we can help with the later stages of formation in which the new idea must be confirmed, refined, and explained to others. Industry analysis is the first of those later stages.

Companies within an industry can affect the market position and financial performance of one another by changes in product design, market segmentation, pricing level, distribution method, advertising effort, production process, technological advancement, and so on. The ability of one firm to affect others is central to the concept of an industry. The automobile industry provides a clear example of the impact one company can have upon others. Japanese car manufacturers entered the U.S. market in the mid-1970s with small, fuel-efficient, and well-built vehicles; they nearly destroyed the traditional American auto companies. The steel industry provides another example. Also during the 1970s, imports of low-priced steel products from European mills captured the markets and reduced the profits of American steel firms; our domestic companies are still reeling from the impact.

The ability of one firm to affect others goes beyond foreign imports and low prices. It may include technological developments, as in Amdahl's design of an advanced computer system which forced IBM to change its product line. It may extend to product promotion, as in Miller Beer's creation of a popular advertising program which altered the market shares of Schlitz and Pabst. Companies within an industry compete on many more dimensions than price. To successfully position a new firm within an industry, you must come to fully understand the historical pattern of competition and probable changes in that pattern.

So far, our examples have featured large companies in traditional industries (autos, steel, computers, and brewing). Larger companies were selected because their names and competitive problems are familiar. Let's examine a much smaller company in a less traditional industry.

Assume you have an idea to teach calculus to high school and college students by using programmed instruction on a personal computer. Further assume you have written the programs for the first five lessons, the programs have been tested at local high schools and at a community junior college, and the instructors at these institutions are enthusiastic about the results. "You ought to start a company," they urged. Now, you are investigating that possibility. What industry are you in?

No existing companies offer computer-based instruction in calculus, but a large number of publishing firms sell textbooks on calculus and an even larger number of software companies provide programs for use on personal computers. You are at the intersection of those two industries because your proposed new product (if it is successfully introduced) will affect both publishing firms and software designers. Your impact will be greater on the publishing firms; your product may replace some textbooks they sell. The software companies may have a greater impact upon you; they can readily develop their own programs to teach calculus.

As you define an industry to analyze, look at the impact one company can have upon others. If you can affect the market position or financial performance of another firm or if they can affect your market position and financial performance, then you are potentially part of their industry and should consider the characteristics of that industry in planning the formation of your company.

Many successful companies are formed at the intersection of two industries. Others are totally contained within the structure of a single industry. Assume, for example, you have an idea for a medium-priced line of gift clothing for preschool children. For a number of years at home you have been making very colorful, easy-to-care-for dresses, shirts, trousers, and jackets for children, aged 2 to 5 years. Your products have been sold in increasingly large numbers each year through a local retail store.

The demand now far exceeds your ability to continue production by yourself. Two other retail stores have offered to carry your products, and you are starting to get inquiries about direct sales from people living in other areas. This is an advanced type of formation problem. You already have much more than just the idea for a new product; you have a developed product line, on-going sales, and satisfied customers.

Your immediate problem is in production: you need a dramatic expansion in capacity. Before you make a large investment in time, effort, and money, examine the childrens' clothing industry to see what long-term competitive advantage you may achieve. You are successful now because of colorful designs and high-quality products. What will

FIGURE 2-1 Participants within an industry.

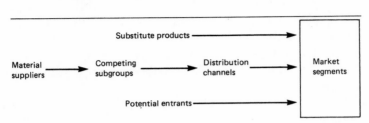

happen if a larger manufacturer copies your designs and sells through discount chain stores? Anticipate such possibilities in the analysis of the industry, comparing the relative competitive positions of your own growing firm and larger manufacturers.

Industry analysis often becomes complex because industries themselves are complex. An industry is more than just the market for products or services of a particular kind plus the companies supplying that market. An industry is composed of a range of market segments[1] for products and services, groups of competing firms that manufacture them, and also includes sources of input supply, channels of output distribution, types of substitute products, and numbers of potential industry entrants. This full view of an industry is shown graphically in Figure 2-1.

Each company within an industry—whether a manufacturer, a distributor, a supplier, a producer of substitute products, or a potential new entrant—can affect the performance and position of other industry firms. A supplier of microelectronic components, for example, can affect the sales of personal computers by making technological advances which reduce the cost and expand the capability of the finished products. A manufacturer of medical diagnostic equipment, similarly, can affect the sales of distributors by starting to sell directly to health care facilities through a company sales force. The firms within an industry are interrelated, and one of the purposes of industry analysis is to develop an understanding of those interrelationships.

All companies within an industry are not equal in size and position.

---

[1] Market segments are groups of customers for a given product or service with identical social, economic, geographic, or behavioral attributes who tend to respond in similar ways to features and functions of the product. See Chapter 3, "Market Planning," for a fuller definition and examples.

A single firm may occupy one or many positions, each determined by differences in product-market orientation, production processes, supply and distribution methods, and so on. Companies within an industry may be vertically or horizontally integrated for example. The vertical dimension refers to stages in production such as raw material processing, part manufacture, subassembly, final assembly, and packaging. The horizontal dimension describes the range of market segments such as those for products varying in price, size, capability, quality, and image.

If you have uncovered a gap in the product line, a niche in the market segmentation, or an opportunity in the production process, you may have identified a new industry position. Why is it currently unoccupied? How will other companies in the industry respond to your sudden appearance in this position?

Alternative positions within an industry and sources of competitive advantage become apparent through analysis of industry "structure." This portrays interrelationships among groups of companies capable of affecting the performance and position of one another by changes in business activities. It is possible to look at industry structure in five dimensions or by making five cuts across the industry on different planes. These dimensions are

1. Market structure, the relationships between product-market positions
2. Production structure, the relationships between product-process methods
3. Economic structure, the relationships between sales revenues, fixed expenses, and variable costs
4. Competitive structure, the relationships between directly competing firms
5. Participant structure, the relationships between the total number of companies within the industry

MARKET STRUCTURE

The market structure of an industry is the pattern of relationships between different product-market positions. For each product there is a corresponding market segment. The term "product-market" is used to describe this relationship. It suggests an interdependency stemming from the match between product attributes and market characteristics.

The market structure of an industry is difficult to explain in plain language. Graphically, it becomes simple. Think of a matrix with product types arranged across the horizontal axis according to some logical order. This ordering could include the basic technologies represented in design, the raw materials used in fabrication, or the store types needed for distribution. On the vertical axis of the matrix, the market segments can be listed according to such logical categories as age brackets, income levels, or residential locations of customers. The result is a chart showing the full range of possible product-market positions within the industry.

To illustrate, we will analyze the men's shirt industry. This is a very competitive industry with many large and established firms. You probably have no intention of forming a new company here, but product types and market segments are easy to envisage. The product-market matrix for the men's shirt industry may be portrayed as in Figure 2-2.

We could, of course, expand the matrix further. Any one of the products listed on the horizontal axis can be subdivided by material (cotton, blend, or synthetic), by weave (oxford, broadcloth, or open), by color (white, blue, or pink), by pattern (striped or checked), and by style (plain or button-down collar). When preparing such a product-market matrix, the intent should be to gain insight into the market structure of the industry. Subdivision by product type or market segment should be carried only so far as additional understanding or insight results.

FIGURE 2-2 Product-market matrix for the men's shirt industry.

| Market segments | Work shirts | | Sport shirts | | Dress shirts | |
	Denim	Flannel	Knitted	Woven	S-sleeve	L-sleeve
High income						
High medium income						
Medium income						
Low medium income						
Low income						

There are no firm rules for dividing either product types or market segments, but matrix cells should be small enough to show clear differences and large enough to be studied when available data are inserted. Data are available, for example, to analyze sales by item for the proposed division of the men's shirt industry. These data, given in Figure 2-3, show some interesting trends between 1972 and 1980.

Obviously, this breakdown of sales by product type provides more useful information than would a summary for the total industry. It is not obvious how much more useful information might be generated by further breakdowns into smaller subdivision, by material, weave, or color. Choice of the best product type and market segment units for analysis of an industry's market structure is a subjective decision, at the discretion of the formation planner. There are no objective rules.

Each cell within a product-market matrix represents a potential competitive position for a company. Except for basic commodity industries such as ore mining or flour milling, the positions tend to differ in overall size, annual growth, competitive intensity, and other factors. In noncommodity industries, an examination should include basic characteristics, competitive entries, and synergistic relationships for each and every cell in the matrix.

1. **BASIC CHARACTERISTICS** of the product-market positions. The basic characteristics include such properties as the total size, annual growth, and historical margins of the cells in the product-market matrix. Not all of these data are readily available, except those for

FIGURE 2-3 Sales data for the men's shirt industry.

Year	Sales, Thousands of units					
	Work shirts		Sport shirts		Dress shirts	
	Denim	Flannel	Knitted	Woven	S-sleeve	L-sleeve
1972	33,709	15,863	8,430	98,688	152,280	308,970
1974	31,744	15,284	12,610	87,792	131,796	279,226
1976	27,264	13,307	16,730	124,524	110,376	292,201
1978	29,790	15,210	34,750	82,644	97,500	259,844
1980	29,021	15,150	54,840	71,532	92,052	262,595

some consumer products whose sales are tracked through distribution channels by private consulting firms or those gathered and published by cooperative industry associations. It may be possible, however, for you to estimate many of the figures, based upon interviews with potential customers, suppliers, and industry analysts. People with extensive experience in an industry often have an intuitive feel for such figures and the product-market trends underlying them.

2. **COMPETITIVE ENTRIES** in the product-market positions. As a second step in the analysis of industry market structure, identify the competing firms and their product entries within each cell of the matrix. Possibly, some cells will have no competitors, indicating either a total lack of demand or a valid gap in the product line or niche in the market segment. Most cells will display a number of competitive entries. Each product entry should be analyzed for market share, design differentiation, and brand reputation and each company marketing plan for pricing level, distribution method, and promotional means. The purpose is to determine which, if any, firm holds a competitive advantage within a particular cell of the matrix and the basis for that competitive advantage. Again, much of the needed information may not be readily available but can be estimated through conducting interviews with people experienced in the industry.

3. **SYNERGISTIC RELATIONSHIPS** between the product-market positions. "Synergy" refers to the appearance of the same company resources in two or more cells of an industry product-market matrix or even in two or more industries. The term is derived from a Greek expression which means working together. Synergy maximizes the productivity of a given resource such as a sales force, a factory building, or a proprietary technology. Use of the same sales force, for example, to sell two different product types in the same market segment or to sell the same product type in two very different market segments, are synergistic approaches.

The concept is appealing. (It is certainly economical to use the same asset or skill twice.) But the application often seems difficult. For meaningful savings to occur, there must be a valid relationship between the cells of a product-market matrix or between the matrices of the industries. In other words, unless the individual customers and the purchasing methods are similar in the two market segments, there will be no savings from using a single sales force; unless the customer motives and buying needs are identical, few economies will accrue from using the same promotional means.

As you plan the formation of your new company within an industry, you should certainly look for synergistic relationships. They may provide substantial competitive advantages either to your new firm or to one of the established competitors. Pay special attention to synergy when considering an apparent gap in the product line or niche in the market segments. Can a competitor, by making minor changes in a product line or giving new directions to a sales force, easily fill the apparent gap or niche? Figures 2-4 and 2-5 show two product-market matrices.

FIGURE 2-4 Product-market matrix for the financial services industry.

Product classification by service types	Market segmentation by income groups					
	Under $20,000	$20,000 to $35,000	$35,000 to $50,000	$50,000 to $75,000	$75,000 to $100,000	Over $100,000
Demand deposits (checking accounts)						
Time deposits (savings accounts)						
Retirement deposits (IRA and Keogh)						
Installment loans (secured)						
Term loans (unsecured)						
Money market funds						
Mutual stock and bond funds						
Individual brokerage services						
Individual trust services						

FIGURE 2-5 Product-market matrix for electrical measuring instruments.

Market segment	Megavolts megaamperes	Kilovolts kiloamperes	Volts amperes	Millivolts milliamperes	Microvolts microamperes	Nanovolts nanoamperes	Picovolts picoamperes
Experimental physics							
Electric power generation							
Consumer appliances							
Consumer electronics							
Communication electronics							
Data processing electronics							
Experimental electronics							

Product classifications by measurement range

PRODUCTION STRUCTURE

The "production structure" of an industry refers to the pattern of relationships between alternative product-process positions within an industry. These product-process positions are not as intuitively understandable as the equivalent product-market positions.

Nearly everyone can list the different market segments which may be targeted for various product types within an industry and consequently prepare a product-market matrix representing all possible product-market positions. It is relatively easy to understand that total size, annual growth, and competitive intensity will probably differ between cells of the product-market matrix and therefore that the sales volume, market share, and brand recognition for individual companies will vary across product-market positions.

The relationship of the product-market position to sales is obvious.

The relationship of a company's product-process position to costs should be equally obvious, but typically it is not.

Costs, of course, are the other half of the margin equation. (Sales revenues minus production costs equal the gross margin—or a company's usual contributions toward selling and administrative expenses plus pretax profits.) Costs are a critical consideration when selecting the competitive position of a new company within an industry. Competitive costs—one firm's costs versus those of others in the same industry—can be studied by looking at the production structure, consisting of alternative product-process positions. Just as the market structure of an industry may be represented by alternative market segments for the various product types, the production structure can be portrayed by alternative production processes for those same products.

There are alternative processes to manufacture nearly every good or service. Each process is associated with a particular unit-output volume, a variable cost figure, and a fixed expense level. The differences between these alternative methods of manufacture lie in physical capacity and process technology.

Larger plants, with greater physical capacity, generally require more investment capital than smaller plants. Larger plants also tend to produce at lower variable costs per unit because of the economies of scale. The problem, of course, is that larger plants usually have higher fixed expenses for interest, depreciation, and taxes. They must operate at capacity or near capacity to be cost effective. The same pattern generally also holds true for modern plants, using advanced technologies.

Plants using advanced technologies typically operate at a lower cost per unit but have a higher fixed expense level, and therefore they must run near capacity. Consequently, two critical decisions in the formation of a high-growth firm are the physical capacity and the technological method to be used in the production process. These decisions frequently are complicated. A single process may be used to produce two or more products. (Remember synergy?) It is necessary to examine the relationships between product-process positions rather than the costs of a single plant. These relationships make up the production structure of the industry.

Production structure also can be portrayed by matrix, with the product types arranged across the horizontal axis according to some logical order. This order probably should parallel that used for the product-market matrix—basic technologies represented in design, raw materials used in fabrication, or store types needed for distribution. On the vertical axis of the matrix, the alternative production processes can be listed, generally in sequence of increasing size or advancing technology. Here, it becomes clear why we selected the men's shirt industry as the primary example for the product-market matrix and now for the product-process matrix. Nearly everyone is familiar with the different market segments and can picture the alternative production processes.

Manufacturing a shirt is a simple process. Cloth—dyed or printed—is cut into flat pieces by following a pattern. The flat pieces are rough-sewn, or "tacked," into shaped parts such as sleeves, collars, or fronts. The shaped parts are then rough-sewn into assembled garments and finally finished-sewn into completed clothing.

Some economies of scale are possible in production, particularly when cutting the cloth into flat pieces: numerous layers can be sliced at one time. There are a few possible applications of technology, also in the cutting operation, in which the patterns can be laid out by computer to minimize waste. Otherwise, shirt manufacturing is a labor-intensive process. As shown in Figure 2-6, it is possible to build five different-sized shirt plants. They would have increasing capital requirements but decreasing unit costs at full capacity.

Just as each cell within the product-market matrix of an industry represents a potential competitive position for a firm, so does each cell within the product-process matrix of the industry. One company can compete in manufacturing—on the basis of plant design, job standards,

FIGURE 2-6 Product-process matrix for the men's shirt industry.

Plant size in units per day	Work shirts		Sport shirts		Dress shirts	
	Denim	Flannel	Knitted	Woven	S-sleeve	L-sleeve
250						
500						
1000						
2000						
5000						

employee effort, and facility utilization—just as readily as it competes in marketing with variables of price level, distribution method, and promotional means.

To compete in manufacturing, you must understand the production structure of the industry—the patterns of volume, cost, and quality relationships among the alternative product-process positions. Once again, this understanding may be achieved by preparing a product-process matrix of the industry and examining each cell in the matrix for basic characteristics, competitive entries, and synergistic possibilities.

While our use of the terms "manufacturing" and "production" may suggest factories producing physical goods, the same concepts are applicable to service firms such as retail stores, wholesale distributors, transportation companies, and consulting agencies. Goods and services are not altogether different. For every successful firm (and this is particularly true for the new firm which must establish a customer base), it is necessary to produce something somebody wants. And it is necessary to produce this good or service in adequate volume, at reasonable cost, and with acceptable quality.

Production, here, refers to volume, cost, and quality for the output of your proposed company, whether it will manufacture industrial parts, assemble consumer products, or produce personal services. Volume, cost, and quality are important competitive tools for high-growth companies. Selection of the most effective production process for each product type depends on your identification of the basic characteristics, competitive entries, and synergistic possibilities within cells of the product-process matrix.

1. **Basic characteristics** of the product-process positions. The basic characteristics of each cell in the product-process matrix include such properties as capacity level, technological method, and cost pattern. These are not easy quantities to measure or even to identify.

   To identify and measure the output capacity of a specific production process for a given product type, for example, you must assume that the process is dedicated to a single product, that the product is a physical good (not a personal or organizational service), and that the good is composed of homogeneous units.

   The capacity of an oil refinery would seem to be measureable in millions of gallons, the capacity of a shirt factory in dozens of shirts.

But the output potential varies with changes in the product mix of gasoline, kerosene, diesel fuel, and heating oil, on the one hand, or work shirts, sports shirts, dress shirts, and women's blouses, on the other.

Most services are difficult to define clearly and impossible to measure exactly. What is the capacity of an accounting firm or an educational program? Both the capacity level and the technological methods are difficult to study except in relative terms, e.g., this plant has greater capacity than that, or this process is more modern than another. Cost is also difficult to study at this stage of the investigation, unless you will be satisfied with relative rather than absolute cost.

Settle for relative information and analyze it. You do not want to start a company based upon a given production process and then find, 6 months later, that your primary competitor has a different production process with a much lower cost structure. Look at the advantages that come with volume increases and those that come with technology changes for each of the alternative production processes.

2. **Competitive entries** in the product-process positions. If you accept the premise that it is possible for companies to compete on the dimensions of plant design, job standards, employee effort, and facility utilization just as they compete through the variables of price, distribution, and promotion in marketing, then also accept the fact that competitive positions in the production structure are important. Each competitive entry within a cell of the product-process matrix should be identified and evaluated for probable capacity, expected costs, and apparent quality. Competitive costs cannot be known, of course. Yet you do know the selling price of competing products. In most industries there is a fairly standard multiplier applied to costs to determine prices. If you can learn what this formula is, you can estimate the production costs of companies within the industry.

3. **Synergistic relationships** between the product-process positions. Synergy, as previously explained, refers to the use of a single resource to support multiple products. In marketing, synergy means the use of the same distribution channel, sales force, or advertising effort for more than one product type. In production, it means the use of the same manufacturing plant, raw material, or labor force for different product types. Synergy in production reduces costs by

providing greater volume at one or more stages in the production process. It can result in significant cost reductions.

A company formed to manufacture men's shirts, for example, might consider adding women's blouses or shirtwaist dresses to gain economies of scale. The potential for synergy should be a major consideration in your investigation of the production structure of an industry. It is easier to achieve full utilization of your production capacity if you have two or more products that can be made interchangeably at the same plant.

ECONOMIC STRUCTURE

The economic structure of an industry refers to the pattern of sales revenues, variable costs, and fixed expenses typical for the industry. Computer software development, for example, is an industry characterized by high fixed expenses. Systems analysts and programmers must be paid regardless of sales performance. Auto parts manufacturing, on the other hand, is an industry marked by high variable costs; marketing and administrative overhead costs normally are minimal.

Each industry has a pattern of revenues, costs, and expenses, although it is not necessary for a new company to adhere to the pattern. Often a company filling a gap in the product line, niche in the market segment, or opportunity in the production process creates a new pattern of revenues, costs, and expenses. This provides a competitive advantage. Fast-food restaurants, which have grown so rapidly over the past 20 years, for example, have a much lower cost structure than others in the restaurant industry because of their semiautomated production processes. This economic advantage is a major reason for their success.

For the benefit of nonaccountants, a "fixed expense" remains constant regardless of production rates; "semi-fixed expenses" vary discontinuously, or in step function, with production; and "variable costs" vary directly with the production rate. In a small machine shop, the foreman's salary would be classified as a fixed expense, the electric bill for both power and light as a semi-fixed expense, and the material used in production as a variable cost. The pattern varies by industry. In a new advertising agency, almost all of the expenses would be fixed; in a security-guard firm, almost all of the costs would be variable.

It is possible to study the pattern of sales revenues, variable costs, and fixed expenses typical for an industry through the mechanics of break-even analysis. The break-even point is the sales volume (in units for a given product or service) at which the total costs, both variable and fixed, are equal to the total revenues. This relationship between sales revenues, variable costs, and fixed expenses can be expressed algebraically or graphically. The graphic representation, shown in Figure 2-7, is easier to grasp.

Break-even analysis is cost-volume analysis. Increases in volume above the break-even point bring decreases in average cost per unit because fixed expenses may be allocated over a larger number of units. These decreases in average unit costs are the economies of scale important for beginning companies. You do not want to start a company to compete against a firm with substantial economies of scale; that would seem obvious. Yet think of the number of companies that have been started to compete against the market leaders in pocket calculators and home computers. None of the new companies have been successful over the long run because of their higher unit costs.

Economies of scale bring increased profit margins and larger production volumes. Yet there is a downside risk. Greater production volumes require larger manufacturing plants, greater capital investments, and higher fixed expenses. If the plants cannot be operated near capacity, economies of scale rapidly disappear. That is why you should look at a full range of possible capacities and alternative tech-

---

FIGURE 2-7 Relationship between sales revenues, variable costs, and fixed expenses.

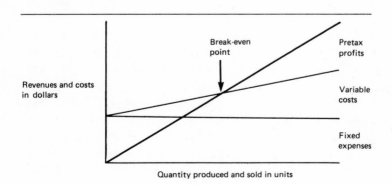

Quantity produced and sold in units

nologies as you evaluate potential product-process positions for your firm.

In addition to economies of scale achieved by increases in the annual production volume, there are economies of experience gained from increases in the cumulative volume of production. In other words, an early market entrant normally will enjoy lower costs per unit than a new competitor entering the same market somewhat later, even though both may produce the same number of units this year. The difference is due to experience gained in production and to the time and effort continually applied to study costs, design tooling, train workers, and improve processes. One large consulting firm claims such a continual effort to study, design, train, and improve will—over time—reduce the direct costs per unit of any good or service in proportion to its cumulative volume; unit costs can be expected to decline by 15 to 20 percent each time cumulative volume is doubled.

Cumulative volume is not annual production rate. Instead, it refers to the total production in units since the beginning of processing for the good or service. The measured decrease in unit costs for each doubling of cumulative volume results in an exponential relationship, shown in Figure 2-8, called the "experience curve."

The decline in average unit cost associated with increases in cumulative volume has been scientifically measured and confirmed for numerous products and services such as microelectronic circuits, mechanical watches, and inorganic chemicals. It is believed this decline results from step-by-step improvements in product design,

---

FIGURE 2-8 Relationship between unit costs and cumulative volume.

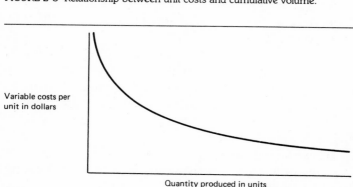

Variable costs per unit in dollars

Quantity produced in units

process methods, and job performances which may be expected to accrue with increasing experience.

The experience curve concept leads to a rule of thumb for the new venture: gain market share quickly, and attempt to dominate the product gap, market niche, or production opportunity you have discovered. The firm with the largest cumulative volume will develop an important cost advantage over all other participants within the industry. This cost advantage may become an important competitive advantage for a new company. When economies of scale are added to economies of experience, the cost advantage may be large enough to dissuade other firms from copying the new product, market, or process concept.

COMPETITIVE STRUCTURE

All firms within an industry do not compete directly against each other. Mercedes Benz and B.M.W. do not compete, except peripherally, against Ford and Chevrolet, although all are participants in the automobile industry. Brooks Brothers does not compete directly against the clothing department of Sears.

Companies within an industry tend to compete in small groups. They tend to form such groups with similar product-market positions and parallel marketing policies (price level, distribution method, and promotional means). Competition, then, occurs primarily among companies within the group, only secondarily affecting other groups within the industry. The beer industry provides a clear example of such competitive groupings. Competition within the brewery industry seems to be based solely on the two dimensions of retail price and advertising expenditures, as depicted in Figure 2-9.

It is important for you as the founder of a new company to identify the competitive groupings of the industry you expect to enter. Except in rare instances, a new company will not be able to enter an industry without competition. Firms in the existing competitive groups will react in different ways to the new product, market, or process concept. You must anticipate those reactions.

Identification of competitive groupings of the industry you expect to enter should be relatively easy. You have, or should have, already charted the product-market position of each company within your ma-

FIGURE 2-9 Competitive groupings in the beer industry.

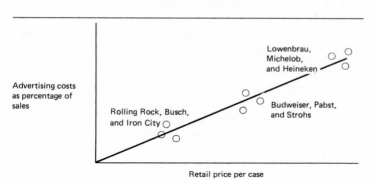

Retail price per case

trix of the industry market structure. Information about the marketing policies of those companies is readily available. Usually, there are three or four firms in each competitive grouping. Examine each of these groupings for degree of competitive intensity and sources of competitive advantage.

COMPETITIVE INTENSITY

The companies within different competitive groupings of an industry do not compete with equal intensity. The amount of competition, measured by the gross margins as a percentage of sales, seems to differ depending upon a number of factors.

1. **Relative size** of the firms in a competitive grouping. Companies of approximately the same size seem to compete more strongly. Firms of substantially different size, with one at least twice the size of the others as measured by sales within the industry, seem to be much more restrained. Perhaps the smaller companies recognize that the larger firm, with economies of scale (and probably of experience), can easily retaliate for any increase in advertising or expansion of distribution.
2. **Annual growth** of the market in a competitive grouping. Companies which serve a static or slowly growing market seem to compete more strongly. Firms serving a rapidly growing market seem to be

less competitive. Perhaps companies in an explosive market recognize that sales growth for one company does not have to be at the expense of others within the industry.
3. **Comparative costs** in a competitive grouping. To a certain extent, this factor parallels the relative size of the firms in the competitive groupings. Larger size is associated with lower costs because of economies of scale and experience. However, it is entirely possible for one firm to have much lower production costs because of advanced technology or more recent construction of manufacturing facilities. Companies with such production cost advantages tend to compete aggressively.

What does competitive intensity mean to an entrepreneur and his or her associates who are thinking about entering an industry with a new product, market, or process concept? It means, on the one hand, that if you will be competing against three or four other firms in approximately the same product-market position and with approximately the same marketing policies and if those other firms are all relatively equal in size and serving a relatively stable market, then you have almost no chance for success. The competitive reactions will be immediate and aggressive. On the other hand, if one of the companies in the grouping is much larger than the others and particularly if the market served by the group is growing rapidly, then competitive reactions may be slower and more subdued.

But, what happens when the new venture grows to a size that is seen as a threat by the larger, older firm? And, what happens when the market reaches maturity and stops growing?

COMPETITIVE ADVANTAGE

All of the companies within a competitive grouping may be equal in size and other resources. They may also perform approximately equally, as measured by financial returns and market growth. Conversely, one of the firms may be performing much better, indicating a competitive advantage of some kind. The founders of a new company—which will take on other companies in a specific grouping of an industry—should carefully assess their competitive advantages and their disadvantages. Both affect the newer firm.

FIGURE 2-10 Chart to compare competitive advantages in an industry.

Area of competitive advantage	Firm A	Firm B	Firm C
1. Product characteristics			
2. Market segments			
3. Price level			
4. Distribution channel			
5. Promotional method			
6. Production process			
7. Plant design			
8. Work-force productivity			
9. Facility utilization			
10. Cumulative experience			
11. Technological level			
12. Invested capital			
13. Sales revenues			
14. Variable costs			
15. Fixed expenses			
16. Available funds			

Prepare a chart, comparing the factors listed in Figure 2-10. In a very competitive industry grouping, all of these factors would be equal; a new company probably should not attempt to enter.

PARTICIPANT STRUCTURE

Participants within an industry include a full array of company types, ranging from firms competing in a given grouping to companies in adjacent groupings to manufacturers of substitute products to potential entrants currently outside the industry—together with suppliers, distributors, and customers. This complete participant structure was previously illustrated in graphic form in Figure 2-1. Refer to it again to make sure you understand their relationships.

Think of industries showing this pattern, including raw material or finished parts suppliers, competitive subgroups, product distributors, and market segments, with the manufacturers of substitute products and the potential entrants into the industry waiting in the wings. Take personal computers, for example. The industry has chip suppliers, computer manufacturers, retail distributors, and finally, customers. Automobiles provide another example. The industry includes part suppliers, car manufacturers, local dealers, and car buyers. All this may seem tedious and dull, but for the founders of a new company it is critically important to know where their firm will be positioned within this chain. Profitability varies widely, depending upon the participant structure of the industry.

In some industries, such as personal computers, the profitability of part suppliers like Intel or Fairchild can be very high; in other industries, such as automobiles, the profitability of part suppliers tends to be very low. It depends upon a factor which, for want of a better name, is called "economic power."

Economic power cannot be measured, but it is easy to understand. It describes the ability of one type of company (within the participant structure of an industry) to impose conditions of purchase or sale upon others. In personal computers, there are a limited number of suppliers of complex integrated circuits, engraved on silicon chips, needed for mathematical functions and numerical memory in the computer. The chip suppliers possess power and profitability equal to that of the manufacturers. In automobiles, there are a large number of suppliers of relatively simple fabricated and machined metal parts. The auto component suppliers enjoy much less power and much lower profitability than the manufacturers.

To some degree, economic power is a function of the relative size of the contending companies within the participant structure of the industry: Large companies tend to have more economic power than small ones. It is also a function of the number of companies within each different group: A smaller number of companies tend to have more economic power than a larger number. Economic power principly refers to the relative impact one company can have upon others. A supplier of cast-iron brake cylinders can have little impact upon General Motors because there are many other sources of supply, including internal manufacturing and substitute materials. General Motors, on the other hand, can have a massive impact upon the foundry selling those cast-iron parts.

Economic power also tends to have an impact upon profitability, as illustrated by the economists' concept of "value added." Value added, quite simply, is the difference between the input material price and the output sales price for companies occupying different positions in the participant structure of an industry, as suggested in Figure 2-11.

Value added refers to the increase in the selling price of a product as it moves through the vertical chain of an industry—from raw material to fabricated part to assembled unit to distributed product. It includes direct costs for labor, power, and depreciation on plant and equipment; indirect charges for supervision, engineering, marketing, and administration; and a remaining amount for profit. Profit tends to mirror the economic power of the company within the industry. To be blunt about this concept of economic power—profit and funds available for engineering, marketing, and administration tend to vary according to the ability of one company within the chain to impose conditions and terms of purchase or sale upon others.

What does economic power mean to the founders of a new company? It is another factor—along with product-market posture, product-process method, economic structure, and competitive grouping—to be considered in positioning a company within an industry. Positions lacking economic power in the participant structure of an industry are often easy to enter. They may require limited capital investment or utilize low technology. They also tend to be relatively unprofitable. You should consider why an apparent gap in the product line, niche in the market segmentation, or opportunity in the production process exists. It may be because no one has hit on the idea previously, or it may be because plenty of people have thought of the idea but none have been

FIGURE 2-11 Value added in the vertical chain of an industry.

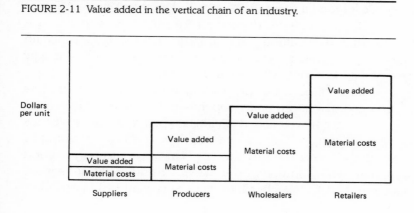

able to make it work because of the economic power relationships in the industry.

Consider, for example, the likelihood that large numbers of people at home have developed new food products such as salad dressings or packaged desserts. These are easy products to develop because of the limited capital and low technology involved. Almost everyone has a kitchen, a stove, and some knowledge about cooking. The problem is: It is almost impossible to obtain distribution. Large chain stores refuse to carry food products produced by smaller firms. The entrepreneur is forced to rely upon small specialty stores for sales and is seldom able to achieve adequate volume for profitable operations. You should not aspire to start a company which will be blocked from achieving profitable operations at the start. Carefully examine the participant structure of the industry for sources of economic power, and beware when those sources are arrayed against you.

Economic power becomes progressively more important to the high-growth firm over the long run. It can block the entrance of subsequent new competitors into an industry and provide barriers to entry which will generate a competitive advantage for your high-growth company. Earlier in this chapter we explained that each new venture needs a reason for success at the start (or a logical reason customers will buy the product or service when it is offered for sale) and a competitive advantage (or a logical reason larger firms will not simply copy the new product or service once it has proven to be successful). Over time, economic power can provide the competitive advantage.

Assume, for example, that despite our explicit recommendation against starting a packaged-food-products company, you have done so. Perhaps you developed a salad dressing with less than one calorie per serving. You called your new dressing Trim. Although you found it difficult to arrange distribution through large chain stores, one chain eventually accepted your product (provided you were willing to pay 70 percent of a cooperative advertising program).

The combination of desirable product features (good taste and low calories), chain distribution, and cooperative advertising has proven successful. Your sales have reached $2,400,000 per year. Your revenues are growing at 40 percent per year, and after-tax profits are running 12 percent of sales. So you say to yourself, "That was certainly a good book on high-growth ventures, with some very useful ideas on marketing, production, and finance, but I am very, very glad I did not follow the authors' advice against starting a business in the packaged-foods industry."

Then one evening, as you are planning your first expansion of distribution territory, your sales manager calls to say that one of the large food-products companies—Kraft, Heinz, or Best Foods—has just announced a new one-calorie salad dressing called Slim. What will happen now?

Look at the competitive advantages. Your new competitor has existing plants to produce and package the new dressing. These plants are scattered throughout the country to reduce freight costs. It has established relationships with national grocery chains. It has a company name recognized by customers, an advertising agency to prepare TV and magazine promotions, and plenty of money to invest in product promotion.

You, on the other hand, have a personal reputation as the inventor of the product, an established relationship with one chain, and some customer loyalty in one region. (Most of your loyal customers will at least try the new competitive product, particularly if it is offered at a somewhat lower price.) This is not a hopeful situation. But do not be discouraged about the prospect of starting a new business.

The possibility of imitation, once your product or market or process concept has been proven, is limited. We picked the one industry—packaged consumer-food products—in which copying is most easy and most common. In other industries copying is much more difficult because it is possible to erect barriers to entry and achieve competitive advantages.

Consider all the sources of economic power as you determine how your company will fit within the participant structure of the industry, both at start-up and several years later when your product, market, or process concept has been proven. There are fifteen possible sources, which are shown in Fig 2-12.

1. **Material supply.** A company which controls the supply of raw materials or fabricated components often has considerable power in the supplying, producing, and distributing chain of an industry. Access to such a supply can provide a competitive advantage, particularly if there is a general shortage of some kind. Chemical companies with access to natural gas at the regulated (lower) price during the 1970s enjoyed a competitive advantage. Electronic firms

FIGURE 2-12 Chart to compare sources of economic power in an industry.

Sources of economic power	Firm A	Firm B	Firm C
1. Material supply			
2. Technological expertise			
3. Product reputation			
4. Brand reputation			
5. Customer loyalty			
6. Distribution access			
7. Promotional ability			
8. Manufacturing plant			
9. Work-force productivity			
10. Facility utilization			
11. Scale economies			
12. Experience economies			
13. Scope economies			
14. Managerial systems			
15. Managerial/technical personnel			

with access to the most advanced memory and processing chips (256K) during the 1980s will achieve a competitive advantage.

2. **Technological competence.** A company which understands the technology better than others in the supplying, producing, and distributing chain of an industry often has considerable power. The fabricators of immensely complex silicon chips needed for mathematical functions and numerical memory in data processing already have been described. A less obvious example would be a company formed to provide consulting to colleges and universities on energy usage and on means of improving the heating and cooling systems on campus. Technical expertise, once developed, can provide a substantial competitive advantage.

3. **Product reputation.** Products can be known for quality of construction, performance, or design, and such a reputation may prove an important source of economic power. Think of consumer products like B.M.W. automobiles, Maytag washers, or Lacoste tennis shirts. Customers demand these goods. Therefore, distributors want to carry them. A reputation for quality in industrial products can be equally valuable. A new venture that can establish a reputa-

tion for product quality will achieve a definite competitive advantage and erect a convincing barrier to entry.

4. **Brand recognition.** Brand recognition differs from product reputation. It refers to widespread customer familiarity with a trade name rather than an acknowledged company reputation for quality. Think of companies such as Hertz, McDonald's, and Sealtest. Customers for both consumer and industrial goods select familiar names over unfamiliar ones, and therefore distributors want to carry them. It is difficult for a new venture to quickly establish brand recognition except through extensive product advertising. Still, it does provide a possible competitive advantage.

5. **Customer loyalty.** Customer loyalty differs from both product reputation and brand recognition. It describes the tendency of some customers to continue buying from the same source not because of product quality or name familiarity but because of a sense of personal obligation. Scientists working in advanced electronics tend to buy test and measurement instruments from the original designers of those instruments as long as the designs are kept current. Probably they believe technological innovation should be rewarded and imitation discouraged. Founders of high-growth companies tend to maintain deposit and loan accounts with the first bank to help them. Apparently, they believe willingness to take a financial risk should be rewarded. Customer loyalty provides economic power within an industry and generates a meaningful barrier to entry.

6. **Promotional message.** Promotional message familiarity is roughly comparable to brand recognition, but with a subtle difference. It is possible for an advertising slogan to become so well known that customers almost automatically ask for that product in preference to other products. Typically, this is limited to consumer products such as Miller Lite beer or Avis car rental. Where it exists, it generates economic power and may provide a barrier to entry.

7. **Distribution access.** All companies do not enjoy equal access to distribution channels. We already have cited common problems of small manufacturers. Some have exclusive contracts with sales representatives and regional dealers, while others have a direct sales force. A new venture—with neither company sales people nor exclusive sales contracts—may find it difficult to become established in an industry. Once established, they will have raised the

barrier somewhat higher for subsequent new entrants to the industry.

8. **Transportation costs.** Products normally have to be moved from the manufacturing site to regional warehouses and then to local dealers or final customers. Distributors often arrange transportation from warehouses to local stores, but generally it is the manufacturer's responsibility to pay for earlier movements from factory to warehouse. Numerous economies are possible—through truckload lots, company vehicles, direct shipments, back hauls, and so on. Transportation economies provide an important source of economic power because they yield better service and lower costs for both distributors and customers. Once a company has established an efficient transportation system, it becomes a powerful barrier to entry.

9. **Manufacturing plant.** One large manufacturing plant built with modern technology or, even better, a series of large manufacturing plants (located to minimize combined production and transportation costs) may provide a potent source of economic power. Companies with modern production technology and dispersed plants usually incur lower direct costs, provided that all plants operate at full capacity. Lower costs than competitors translates into considerable economic power and a high barrier to entry.

10. **Work-force productivity.** Worker productivity will vary, even between companies in the same industry. These variations may be due to geographic differences, local traditions, employment policies, union restrictions, or other factors. Worker productivity can be a source of competitive advantage for many smaller firms because of close relationships between owners, managers, and workers. Output per employee-hour and attention to quality tend to be higher.

11. **Facility utilization.** A company that can utilize physical facilities more fully than others within the industry generally will enjoy lower costs and a competitive advantage. Airlines prefer to dispatch airplanes with a full load. Accounting firms like to keep their junior accountants and auditors fully occupied. Full utilization leads to lower costs and consequently to economic power and barriers to entry.

12. **Scale economies.** High annual output volume typically yields lower costs—through economies of scale. And lower costs create

one of the most meaningful barriers to entry within an industry. It is difficult to compete against another firm if their costs are lower than your own; they accumulate a large margin to spend on product development, advertising, and promotion. The founders of a new venture should carefully consider which company within the industry is likely to have the greatest scale economies in 3 to 5 years. Probably you should not start your venture unless you are reasonably certain it will be your own firm.

13. **Experience economies.** High cumulative volume also generally leads to lower costs—from the experience curve effect. Costs do not automatically come down; they have to be driven down by product redesign, improved tooling, worker training, and other advancements. Experience economies generate a reliable barrier to entry and a renewable competitive advantage. Pocket calculators, personal computers, and microelectronic components each illustrate the effects of the learning curve. Again, as the founder of a new venture, you should consider which company within the industry will achieve the greatest experience economies in 3 to 5 years, and you should then work energetically to make certain it will be your own firm.

14. **Managerial systems.** Established systems for planning, control, and motivation provide a competitive advantage. It is difficult to compete against a firm which plans sales growth, controls production costs, and motivates marketing and manufacturing employees for a sustained effort. Development of managerial systems take time, but once in place those systems can improve performance. Continually improving performance creates a barrier to entry for other firms within the industry.

15. **Company culture and managerial style.** The culture of an organization and the style of its managers are difficult to define. Yet they exist, and they influence the performance of a firm. Once again, it takes time to develop a culture and a style. Many firms never accomplish it. Company culture and style can provide a competitive advantage for a new company within an industry.

We believe industry analysis is an essential first step toward fitting a new venture into an industry. Each industry has a market structure, a production structure, an economic structure, a competitive structure, and a participant structure. The founders of a new company have to understand those relationships within the industry. The next step should be to select a product-market position; a product-process position; and a sales-revenues, fixed-expenses, variable-costs position, all of which will combine to create a competitive advantage against current competitors and barriers to entry against future competitors. Starting a high-growth company is a risky, uncertain endeavor, but it becomes much more certain once the sources of competitive advantage are known. Industry analysis is the search for competitive advantages.

Once you have positioned the new company within the industry (to maximize competitive advantages over the immediate future and the long run), next you must implement this position through development of a marketing plan, a production plan, a financial plan, and an organizational plan. The next four chapters will describe each of these specialized planning processes.

CHAPTER THREE
MARKET
PLANNING

The marketing plan for a start-up venture should be based upon the product-market position selected by the founders after making a competitive analysis of the industry. In your analysis, you proposed a product with certain characteristics and identified a market with known attributes. The marketing plan for your firm must be built upon those characteristics and attributes.

The characteristics of the product and the attributes of the market, together, determine the process through which people decide to buy or not to buy your product. Computer engineers evaluating a new software program, for example, follow a different decision path than family members selecting a clothes dryer or teenagers considering a rock album. Analyze this process—and the underlying needs and wants which shape your customers' buying motives—before setting the price level, arranging the distribution channels, and choosing the promotional means. Price, distribution, and promotion plans must fit your customers' buying decision process. They result in a comprehensive marketing plan with an expected sales volume, market share, and expense level.

Market planning is not what some people fear it will be: customer exploitation. It is something entirely different. You start with a worthwhile product, having clearly identified features and fuctions that people in a known market segment want to buy. Then you set the price at a level those people are willing to pay, offer it for sale at places they find convenient to get to, and inform them about the product by means they feel are interesting and appropriate. Sound market planning should help your prospective customers, not entrap them.

To set the price at the right level, distribute the product by the proper channels, and promote it by the best means, you must understand the needs, wants, and motives of your customers and the steps in the purchasing process. These customer inclinations and activities relate to the characteristics of the product and the attributes of the market. The relationships in a marketing plan are shown graphically in Figure 3-1.

A start-up venture has more control over some components in the marketing plan than others. It has only partial control over the product-market variables for example. You can position your company in a given product-market cell or set of cells in the chosen industry, but the size of the market segment is influenced by social and economic trends in the environment over which you have no control.

The characteristics of your product line are the result of a research and development process which may or may not be fully successful. Developers of computer-based games, for example, strive for realistic settings and interactive characters, but so far they have been unable to fully achieve those design objectives. The product-market position can be considered a semi-decision variable, only partially under the control of the firm.

Demand variables of the marketing plan are completely outside the control of the company. The demand variables include customer motives for buying a product or service, customer needs or wants potentially satisfied by purchasing that product or service, and the different stages and participants in the purchasing process. None of these can be controlled. Operators of real estate firms might wish that both partners in a marriage did not have to agree before buying a new house, and they doubtless would prefer that their customers did not

FIGURE 3-1 Relationships among market planning variables.

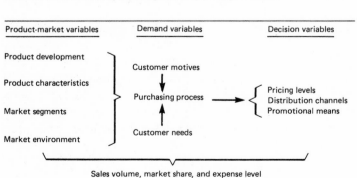

Product-market variables	Demand variables	Decision variables
Product development	Customer motives	Pricing levels
Product characteristics	Purchasing process	Distribution channels
Market segments		Promotional means
Market environment	Customer needs	

Sales volume, market share, and expense level

want to examine different models at various locations before reaching a joint decision, but company actions cannot change these demand variables.

Other decision variables—those for pricing, distribution, and promotion—are completely within the control of the company. Founders of a firm can change pricing levels, distribution channels, and promotional methods at will according to their evolving concept of an effective marketing plan for a given product or service.

The combination of decision variables (within the control of the company), demand variables (outside the control of the company), and product-market position (partially under the control of the company) suggests that marketing management—which begins with the development of the market plan—is both an art and a science. Personal imagination and innovation are just as necessary for successful market planning as analytical methods and techniques. For the beginning firm this is often advantageous; entrepreneurs and close associates usually are better at using their imagination and harnessing innovation than they are at implementing analytical methods and techniques.

A complete marketing plan, conceived through imagination, innovation, and analysis, consists of the ten components given in Figure 3-1. Each of these components will be described. They are applicable to large and small companies alike; to consumer and industrial products; to manufacturing, wholesaling and retailing firms; and to start-up ventures. In developing your marketing plan, consider these ten components in the same sequence as they are presented here. This will help you to discover the relationships among them.

PRODUCT CHARACTERISTICS

A product is commonly thought of as a physical object which is manufactured and then offered for sale. Soap, cosmetics, cars, and clothing are all products of this kind. So are industrial machines, office supplies, and medical equipment.

In marketing terms, *anything which a seller can offer to a buyer is called a product*. Raw materials such as coal, wool, or foodstuffs are products in this sense. Consumer services such as appliance repairs, hair cuts, and television programs also can be considered products.

Commercial services such as public accounting, data processing, or management consulting qualify as products, too. A product, in other words, is anything expected to yield satisfaction and benefit to a buyer, and therefore it may be offered for sale.

The first step in the design of a marketing plan is to specifically identify the features and functions of a product which yield satisfactions and benefits to the prospective buyer. The features (what a product is) may be tangible or intangible; the functions (what a product does) seem halfway between tangible and intangible.

1. **Tangible features** are objective evaluations of product characteristics. These include the physical features of the product, such qualities as appearance, size, composition, color, and shape. How does the product feel and smell? What are its technical specifications? Is it easy to handle, convenient to use, and simple to demonstrate? Will it wear well? Can it be easily repaired? Answers to these questions can be found by examining the product; they constitute its tangible features. Tangible, of course, means physical and subject to examination by our senses of sight, smell, taste, touch, and hearing.

2. **Semi-tangible functions** combine objective and subjective evaluations of product performance. What does the product do? What are the actual results of using the product?

   Toothpaste, to offer a familiar example, has the tangible features of being a soft, partially-abrasive cleaning compound with a given color and taste. The semi-tangible functions of toothpaste are that it cleans teeth, freshens breath, and prevents cavities. These functions can be observed by our physical senses, but they cannot be accurately measured or definitely related to the use of the product. Clean teeth typically do appear whiter than unclean teeth, but it is hard to measure whiteness; tooth appearance is dependent upon many other factors than the type and amount of toothpaste used.

3. **Intangible features** are subjective evaluations of the use of a product. What do buyers think the product will do for them, beyond the semi-tangible functions? What are the personal results of using the product? Toothpaste is advertised as creating popularity for teenagers, romance for young adults, and success for middle-aged persons; the prevention of cavities is stressed only for young children, whose parents actually buy the product.

Down-filled jackets provide another example of the differences between the three types of product characteristics. Tangible features of the jackets include their size, style, color, fabric, and insulating qualities; a semi-tangible function is keeping the wearers warm in cold weather without being heavy; and the intangible features include their association with downhill skiing, mountain climbing, wilderness camping, and other outdoor activities considered glamorous and exciting. People in relatively warm climates have been buying down jackets, probably because they are fashionable not because they are resistant to the cold.

The new "thinsulate" jackets add the tangible feature of being warm without being bulky and the intangible features of being stylish and slim. They sell at a considerable premium over the down jackets—not because they are warmer, but because they enable the buyer to look thinner and more athletic. Do not neglect intangible product features in developing your marketing plan.

The tangible and intangible features and the semi-tangible functions of a product differentiate that product from competing items. "Product differentiation" refers to differences in physical characteristics and performance qualities of, and personal beliefs about, various similar products. The tangible features of size, weight, and horsepower; the semi-tangible functions of speed, comfort, and safety; and the intangible features of luxury and style, for example, differentiate a Cadillac from a Plymouth or Volkswagen. Product differentiation is an important element of the marketing plan, particularly for consumer items. Yet not all products can be differentiated.

Basic raw materials such as coal, sugar, or lumber are generally considered to be undifferentiated commodities. Standard manufactured goods such as capscrews, radiators, or pencils are not commodities but, nevertheless, are thought to be relatively undifferentiated.

All products, except for the most basic materials, have some features or functions which distinguish them from the competition. For a start-up firm, it is critically important to clearly identify the characteristics—tangible, semi-tangible, and intangible—of the product, paying special attention to features and functions which provide some differentiation from the competition. Product characteristics yielding competitive differences are essential to effective market planning for a high-growth company.

PRODUCT DEVOLOPMENT

The characteristics of a product are not irrevocably fixed. Product features and functions may be changed to adapt them to trends in the market environment, to variations in customer motives, or to challenges from competitive producers. A second step in the development of a complete marketing plan is to consider the need for design changes or design modifications which improve product characteristics.

For a start-up venture with limited resources, only design modifications are feasible, and these have to be limited. Product characteristics must fit the needs and wants of the customers at the very beginning. Later, there can be some product modifications—one at a time as customers suggest them—to help increase sales. Most new companies lack the money and the staff to accomplish major design changes.

Major design changes should be anticipated over the long run. Your new product line, no matter how innovative and advanced it now may be, will someday mature. And that will be the time for further research and development. The issue, however, should be considered a minor one in formation planning. At this stage, your attention must be focused totally on getting the company started. Design changes—always interesting to people with technical expertise—have to be set aside until the company is operating profitably enough to pay for them.

MARKET SEGMENTS

Market segments are groups of prospective customers with identical socioeconomic, geographic, or behavioral attributes who tend to respond in similar ways to product features and functions. In short, market segments are composed of the most likely customers for a given product or service.

The total number of potential customers for any product or service, theoretically, is the national population—230 million people of all ages, sexes, incomes, occupations, locations, and so on. This primary market can be divided into secondary market segments by age, sex, income, and other classification measures, singling out groups more likely to purchase a specific product or service.

Large primary markets of all kinds can be divided into smaller secondary segments. For example, the primary market for womens' dresses could be represented by everyone within the United States. (Certainly, some men purchase dresses as presents.) A more realistic view would be to define the primary market as the female population.

To isolate various secondary segments, we merely narrow the focus further. Because dresses differ by style, it may be necessary to specify an age group; as they differ by price, it may be necessary to identify an occupation; and because they differ by warmth, it may be necessary to consider geographic location. A dress designed for sale to professional women aged 25 to 34 with a high family income and a residence in the northern states, for example, would be very different from a dress designed for sale to women aged 45 to 54, who worked mainly in the home with much lower family income and a residence in southern California.

Primary markets can be divided into secondary segments along a number of dimensions. These dimensions may be classified as socioeconomic, geographic, and behavioral attributes.

1. **Socioeconomic attributes** for market segmentation include such factors as age, sex, income, occupation, education, family size, ethnic group, religious affiliations, political attitudes, and leisure activities. These attributes focus on the identity of members of the market segment: Who are they?
2. **Geographic attributes** for market segmentation include such factors as region of the country (northeast, mid-Atlantic, etc.), density of population (urban, suburban, or rural), size of city, and type of climate. These attributes focus on the location of members of the market segment: Where do they live?
3. **Behavioral attributes** for market segmentation include such factors as usage rate, brand loyalty, channel allegiance, and price sensitivity. These attributes focus on the character of members of the market segment: What are they like?

A combination of socioeconomic, geographic, and behavioral attributes should be used to clearly identify secondary market segments. Precise identification of prospective customers is one of the most basic tasks in the development of a marketing plan for a beginning firm. Founders of the new company should know the attributes of people likely to buy their products—whether those products are raw materials, personal services, or manufactured goods and whether they are intended for consumer or industrial use. In other words, you must single out your customers, learn what they want, why they want it, and how they may be willing to buy it from you.

MARKET ENVIRONMENT

The market environment is the full array of demographic, economic, social, political, and competitive forces influencing the demand for a company's products. These forces reflect the national scene and business community within which a company markets its particular goods or services.

Forces emanating from the market environment, as previously explained, are completely outside the control of the firm. Economic trends such as recession or inflation cannot be reversed by company actions. Demographic and social shifts such as the increasing age of the population and the rising status of women also cannot be changed by the firm. Such forces are called primary demand factors because they may alter the composition (number of people) and attributes (characteristics of people) of primary market segments. These factors have to be considered as you develop your marketing plan.

1. **Demographic demand factors** include the increasing population totals, changing age structures, shifting religious and ethnic percentages, and moving residential centers. The composition of the national population—measured by age, sex, ethnic origin, and religious affiliation—is constantly changing, and these changes vary by geographic area and economic class. A complete marketing plan requires frequent updates in response to such trends.

2. **Economic demand factors** include dwindling increases in gross national product; shifting levels of personal and disposable income; varying rates of inflation, interest, and employment; sweeping changes in the supply of and demand for energy, raw materials, and skilled labor; and decreasing productivity in basic manufacturing and repair services. These trends deliver different impacts in different regions of the country and upon different social and economic groups. A complete marketing plan must acknowledge these impacts.

3. **Social demand factors** include rising educational levels, changing employment patterns, and altered social roles. During the past
several decades, we have witnessed substantial shifts in attitudes
about minority rights, individual responsibilities, life styles, and social values. These changes also vary by geographic area and income
class and must be considered in a complete marketing plan.
4. **Political demand factors** include the existing welfare system,
shrinking urban services, threatened Social Security, and expanding
military expenditures. The government—at federal, state, and local
levels—is both a customer and a regulator. Government purchases
are so large, even for nonmilitary items, they form separate, new
market segments. Government regulations are so important, especially in health and environmental fields, they also create new market segments. Government policies are so pervasive, governing both
procurement and regulation, they ultimately have an impact on vir-
tually all market segments. Considerations of these policies and the
underlying political forces from which they originate have to be
included in a complete marketing plan.

Adjustment to demographic, economic, social, and political changes
in the market environment should become one of the strengths of the
beginning firm. A start-up venture does not have established price
levels, distribution channels, or promotional means and therefore can
develop a marketing plan reflecting current trends which influence
customer needs and wants and the purchasing process.

PURCHASING PROCESS

The purchasing process refers to the stages in a typical decision to buy
a product or service, to the people who participate in that decision,
and to the conditions surrounding the decision. Elements of the purchasing process vary along logical continuums between consumer and
industrial products and between disposable and capital goods. Many
more family members will participate in the decision to buy a new car,
for example, than in the decision to try a new detergent, and much
more time will be spent in examining alternatives to a steel blast

furnace than to an office typewriter. Regardless of the purchasing situation, however, the principles remain the same.

There are predictable stages in reaching all purchasing decisions. There are expected participants in those decisions. There are foreseeable conditions affecting them. These stages, participants, and conditions must be analyzed and included in the marketing plan.

1. **Stages in the purchasing process** include felt need, prepurchase comparison, purchase choice, product use, and post-use reactions. People first have to decide they want or need a product, whether it is a consumer or industrial good. Next, a period of comparison among alternative products usually follows, although this may be shortened by brand loyalty, sales promotion, or personal recommendations. After the actual purchase, there comes eventual use and personal reaction to the features and functions of the product.

   All products are expected to yield satisfactions and benefits to the buyer. These expectations may or may not be met: Reactions may be positive, negative, or mixed. Such reactions, of course, have a cumulative impact upon continued sales.

2. **Participants in the purchasing process** for consumer goods include family members and friends who may advise on the purchase and use of the product; for industrial items, the engineering, manufacturing, and financial personnel who may assist in the purchase and use. Both advice and assistance may be extended by these participants at any of the five stages in the purchasing process.

3. **Conditions in the purchasing process** include the normal time, place, and frequency of purchase; delivery method; and payment terms. It is no secret that food items are purchased in a grocery store, for cash and automobiles in a dealership, often for credit. Yet these customer expectations about the location and terms of sale are important—at all stages and for all participants in the purchasing process. These expectations have to be assessed and included in the marketing plan.

CUSTOMER NEEDS AND WANTS

Customer needs and wants trigger the purchasing process; they provide the reasons people buy products and services. In marketing terms, customer needs and wants are the expectations of benefits and satisfactions which a company seeks to satisfy by offering a product with specific features and functions for sale to members of a given market segment.

A useful distinction can be made between needs and wants. Needs are basic, permitting choice only on the manner in which they are met. At the most fundamental level are human needs for food, warmth, and shelter from the extremes of weather; if these are not met, a person cannot survive. Defense against violence and theft and acceptance in the family and community are also needed by most people. Similarly, various kinds of businesses have basic needs which must be met: a plumber's tools; a retailer's inventory; and a railroad's engines, railcars, and tracks.

Beyond such basic needs, there are all the other manufactured goods which people or companies would like to own and all the personal services which they would like to receive. In marketing terms, these nonbasic or optional expectations of benefits and satisfactions are called "wants." Given this distinction, it can be said that a person needs shoes, but wants a tennis racket; a business office may need additional desks, but members of the management may want better parking spaces.

People generally will satisfy their needs before their wants. It would seem to follow that a product that meets customers' needs would be easier to sell than one that meets only their wants. In the real world, however, a specific product often meets the needs of some people and the wants of others. A wrench meets the needs of a plumbing contractor, for example, but satisfies the wants of a homeowner who likes to keep handy tools around the house. A television set meets the needs of a family lacking other entertainment alternatives, but satisfies a want for the person who only likes to watch the evening news program.

To some extent, a close examination of customer needs and wants is a more appropriate marketing activity for an established business in a mature industry (in which these needs and wants will be reflected in advertising) than for a beginning company in a growing market. For the start-up venture, the essential issue is to understand the reasons why customers will purchase your product. Put yourself in the place of a customer, and try to imagine his or her needs and wants.

Entrepreneurs often find it difficult to dissociate themselves from their products and from their pride in ownership. "This is my product," you may say to yourself. "It is designed with a new technology or developed for a new market or manufactured by a new process. Of course, everyone will want to buy it." This seems to be a common attitude and a common failing. We strongly recommend—that for at least one day—the founders of a new company put themselves in the place of their prospective customers. Try to imagine their needs and wants, to anticipate their method of purchase, and to understand their motives. It is a worthwhile exercise which will help you to develop an effective marketing plan.

CUSTOMER MOTIVES

Customer motives underlie the "decision methods" used to evaluate personal needs and wants by individual purchasers. Such decision methods are the analytical techniques people use to make up their minds before purchasing a product or service.

Each customer in a given market segment has personal needs and wants which may or may not be satisfied by the purchase of a certain product or service. Each product or service of a given type, on the other hand, has apparent features and functions which may or may not satisfy those personal needs and wants.

During the purchasing process, customers use some method to compare their needs and wants with the product's features and functions. This method or technique is usually not just a simple feature-by-feature and function-by-function comparison of available goods and services. (There are too many goods and services on the market; the features and functions of the products often are not obvious; and the needs and wants of the customers often are not clear.) Instead, customers use both rational and irrational methods of comparison, and both kinds of methods are termed "customer motives."

The distinction between customer motives and customer needs or wants may be made clearer with an example. Imagine two people in a clothing store, with exactly the same demographic backgrounds (age, sex, income, occupation, education, ethnic group, and family status). Both have decided to buy a new sweater, and both already possess plenty of other clothing; therefore they are concerned more with their desire for esteem and respect from others than with their need for protection from the cold. One of them may buy a sweater because it is on sale, however, and the other because it is heavily advertised. Obviously, there is a difference here in the outcome of the purchasing process, and this difference can be explained by customer motives.

The first customer compared his or her needs and wants for a sweater to the features and functions offered by a range of sweaters and made a decision based upon economic value. The second made the same comparison, but made a decision based upon brand familiarity. The needs and wants were similar, but the decision methods or customer motives were different.

As was suggested earlier concerning detailed analysis of needs and wants, a detailed investigation of customer motives is probably more appropriate for an established business in a mature industry than for a beginning firm in a growing market. For the new company it is important to recognize only that standards of evaluation (which customers will use to compare your product with those of your competitors) are not necessarily economic.

Many entrepreneurs believe it is essential to set the lowest price absolutely or the lowest price relative to some measure of performance. Perhaps it will prove more important to achieve the greatest assurance of service, the best reputation for precision, or even the highest brand name recognition. Customers are not always economically rational; they make decisions based upon personal objectives and group opinions just as we all do.

PRICING LEVEL

Selection of the pricing level is the first true decision variable of the marketing plan to be considered thus far. Others, as previously explained, are selection of the distribution channel and promotional means. All three are completely under the control of the company. The founders of a start-up venture can set the price, establish distribution, and begin advertising based upon their understanding of product characteristics, market attributes, and other influences on the purchasing process.

Pricing is not necessarily the most important of the three decision variables, although it does influence the potential size of the total market and determines the financial contribution of the product line (sales revenues minus variable costs of production). Price should be thought of as part of a package consisting of price, distribution, and promotion. These three variables, considered jointly, are often called the marketing "mix."

Pricing is seldom a scientific procedure. The equilibrium or theoretically correct market price cannot be known, except for widely traded commodities such as wheat or coal or for highly competitive products such as capscrews or breakfast cereals. It is unlikely that many high-growth firms will be started to sell widely traded commodities or highly competitive products, however. Therefore, we recommend start-up ventures use one of three pragmatic pricing methods.

1. **Multiplied cost pricing.** Prices may be set at computed levels to generate a standard percentage above costs (markup pricing) or a standard return on investment (target pricing). Companies which dominate a market (such as General Motors in automobiles before the advent of Japanese competition or General Electric in motors and controls) usually set their prices at a known multiplier of their costs.

2. **Perceived value pricing.** Prices may be set at intuitive levels to reflect scarcity and the value customers place upon products with unique or advanced characteristics. Companies which achieve technological breakthroughs (such as IBM in computers and Polaroid in cameras) and companies which sell art objects and antique furniture often use perceived value pricing.

3. **Expected share pricing.** Prices may be set at competitive levels to maintain an existing market share or at slightly below competitive levels (predatory pricing) to gain market share and forestall competition. Companies that do not dominate a market (such as Chrysler in automobiles or Westinghouse in electric motors and controls) generally must set their prices at levels established by the largest competitors to maintain their market share in the industry.

DISTRIBUTION CHANNEL

Selection of the distribution channel is the second decision variable which contributes to a marketing mix of price, distribution, and promotion. Distribution initiates and maintains contacts between producer and purchasers for the transfer of both physical goods and market information. Goods and services move up the channel, and information and payments move back down. The start-up company needs the down-flow (information and payment procedures) fully as much as it needs the up-flow (distribution of its products and services).

The selection of the most effective distribution channel also is rarely a scientific process. For the beginning firm, dominant concerns are usually distribution cost and customer contact.

Distribution methods generating the most extensive customer contacts, unfortunately, tend to be most expensive. Thus, the distribution decision for a start-up venture is often an unsatisfactory compromise. In reaching this compromise, company founders should consider the types of available distribution channels and the functions they want those channels to perform.

1. **Types of distribution channels** range from personal contacts between the producer and the customer (direct sales) to those involving one, two, or even three intermediaries (indirect sales through retailers, wholesalers, and jobbers). Most industrial materials sold in large quantities to a limited number of users flow up a direct channel of distribution, and consumer goods sold in small volumes to a large number of customers move through wholesalers and then retailers. Usually, direct distribution is more expensive than indirect, although commissions and discounts charged by wholesalers, retailers, and manufacturers' representatives can be substantial. The reason direct distribution often costs more is that sales expenses are fixed in the form of salaries and travel allowances. Thus, the beginning firm typically selects the variable costs of indirect sales despite its lack of direct contact with customers.

2. **Functions of distribution channels** range from sales contacts and order write-ups to the transportation, storage, delivery, installation, and repair of goods and the supervision of credit. For direct industrial sales, the producer generally is responsible for all of these functions; for indirect consumer sales, the responsibilities are typically divided among the intermediaries, although occasionally they are completely neglected (repair service at most retailers, for example). Many start-up firms use manufacturers' representatives; the division of responsibilities may follow industry tradition or result from specific negotiations.

PROMOTIONAL METHOD AND MESSAGE

Selection of the promotional method and message is the third and last of the decision variables which should be taken jointly. Price, distribution, and promotion must work together. For example, it is alleged that wholesalers, retailers, and manufacturers' representatives (most of whom carry a large number of different products) make a very limited effort to sell any particular good or service. This may be especially true for goods or services produced by small firms which have limited economic power in the marketplace. This lack of "push" through the distribution channel results in a need for greater "pull" through the promotional means, and the consequent greater expense for advertising creates a need for a higher price. Thus, the three decision variables must be interrelated in the marketing mix.

Promotion, as one ingredient in the marketing mix, provides a point of contact between the producer and the customer outside the channels of distribution. It transfers information about the product and reminds people about the company. The most basic promotional method is advertising (visual, written, or spoken messages published for a fee in commerical media). But there are other means such as coupons and price rebates to consumers, discounts and sales incentives for distributors, display materials provided at the point of sale (stores or trade shows), and public relations in the form of press releases. Advertising remains the major promotional method, however. There are three principle considerations in developing an advertising program for a start-up venture.

1. **Advertising expenditures.** The amount to be spent on advertising by established companies is usually calculated as a percentage of expected sales; for a beginning firm, the amount spent has to be considered an initial investment. High-growth companies often are short of money at the start, and advertising is one of the optional expenses frequently curtailed. This may become a tragic mistake. The promotional effort should depend upon the design of the marketing plan and not on the limitation of funds.
2. **Advertising media.** Methods to be used in advertising include direct mail, daily newspapers, popular magazines, trade journals, radio stations, and television programs; these vary greatly in cost

and impact. An established firm can select the proper method, or combination of methods, based upon prior sales responses to specific advertising efforts. A start-up venture does not have this experience, of course, and has to rely on computing the advertising cost per consumer contact and then estimating the impact of that contact. When using direct mail advertising, for example, a rule of thumb suggests a response rate of 1 to 2 percent is normal. Thus, 50 or 100 customer contacts may be required to generate a single sale.

3. **Advertising message.** The message to be carried by advertising may stress characteristics of the product line; attributes of the market segment; needs, wants, or motives of the prospective customers; or information about prices and distribution. Most beginning firms rely on advertising agencies to develop the messages but often come away disappointed by the dull, unimaginative proposals received; advertising agencies tend to assign their most creative people to their largest accounts. We strongly recommend that the founders of a new company prepare their own messages, stressing the important features and functions of their product.

The marketing plan should document and justify a set of decisions which interrelate price level, distribution channel, and promotional method. These decisions should be based upon analyses of the needs and wants of prospective customers, their motives for purchase, and the stages and participants in the buying process. These analyses, in turn, should be tied to an understanding of the tangible and intangible characteristics of your product line and the personal and behavioral attributes of your chosen market segment. The relationships in a marketing plan are the key to its success and may be emphasized for the founders of a new company by looking again at Figure 3-1 at the beginning of this chapter.

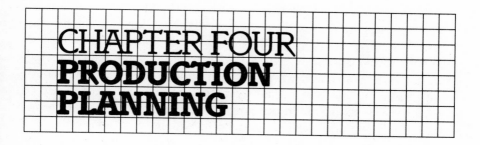

CHAPTER FOUR
PRODUCTION PLANNING

The production plan is built upon the product-process position identified in industry analysis. The product-process position suggests specific elements of your product design—known features and functions—and a processing method with a given capacity, using a particular technology. The production plan helps convert this general picture of how you might go about making your product into a map of physical facilities through analysis of operational variables. Then it considers task variables and quantitative methods needed to manage your company facilities at a prescribed output volume, cost level, and quality standard. Relationships among the components of a complete production plan are shown graphically in Figure 4-1.

FIGURE 4-1 Relationships among production planning components.

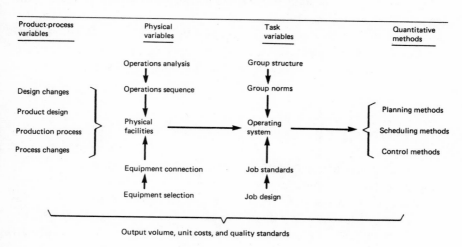

The production plan leads new company founders to design a system for producing a chosen good or service, to determine the tasks of people who will operate the system, and to establish scheduling and control mechanisms for optimal performance. Traditionally, production has been associated with the factory and with the design, scheduling, and control of large-scale manufacturing processes. Because of the increasing economic importance of service industries and the increasing need to improve productivity and quality throughout the U.S. economy, principles and techniques of production management have been extended to such nonfactory settings as retail stores, financial offices, and wholesale distributors and to such nonbusiness establishments as educational institutions, health care facilities, and governmental units. As a result of these recent alterations in our national economy, production management for any organization can now be defined as increasing output while reducing costs and improving quality. It does not matter whether your particular company is devoted to providing consumer services or to manufacturing physical goods. Increasing output while reducing costs and improving quality is universally important to the beginning firm. Output volume, unit costs, and quality standards each make a noticeable impact upon the marketing and financial performance of a company.

A complete production plan, as illustrated in Figure 4-1, includes fifteen components. Components of production management, like marketing management, are applicable to large and small companies; to consumer and industrial products; to manufacturing, wholesaling, and retailing firms; and to start-up ventures. Yet, you should recognize the product or service differences implied by these various categories. Whatever your category may be, consider each component in sequence to develop an overall production plan for your new company.

PRODUCT DESIGN

A product was previously defined as any raw material, personal service, or physical good which might be expected to yield satisfactions and benefits to a buyer and therefore may be offered for sale. Characteristics of the product yielding those satisfactions and benefits were further defined as features (what a product is) and functions (what a product does).

Product design is the creation-in-idea-form of a material, service, or good to provide particular features and functions. Consequently, the first step toward the development of your production plan must be to specify exactly what features and functions you want to achieve through product design. A start-up firm cannot afford the consumer and distributor problems inherent in setting different specifications for manufacturing and marketing the same product. Both dimensions should match precisely.

DESIGN CHANGES

Product engineering goes a step further than design and considers how components of the product are to be made and assembled most efficiently. Engineers critically review design components one by one to determine which can be standardized and which can be simplified to improve the production process—without changing market specifications.

1. **Standardization** refers to the reduction of variations in your material, service, or good to gain uniformity and interchangeability. It is easier to make uniform products and assemble interchangeable parts. Since uniform products and interchangeable parts are normally manufactured in volume by mass-production techniques, the concept of standardization is often believed to be applicable only to large manufacturing firms in basic industries. Standardization is equally useful in smaller companies and service organizations.

   Quick-service restaurants, for example, rely upon the time and cost savings of standardized food servings. Specialized retail stores such as tall girl shops gain inventory and space savings from stocking a standardized range of sizes.
2. **Simplification** means exactly what you think it does: reduction of product or service complexities to achieve easier processing methods. Simplification may include substitution of materials, relaxation of tolerances, and combination of operations. It is often easier to make products from plastic than from steel for example. Plastic parts may be molded as a unit and require no assembly.

   Since simplification is often illustrated by examples from metalworking machine tools, it is sometimes believed the concept is applicable only to large manufacturing firms which use such equipment. It is equally applicable to smaller companies and service organizations.

A large share of automated data processing services are derived from the simplification of manual bookkeeping for example. Many operations are combined into a single process.

Overnight package delivery, likewise, is the simplification of normal freight service. It substitutes methods (aircraft for heavy trucks) and combines operations (central area sorting).

PRODUCTION PROCESS

The production process specifies a capacity in units per hour, day, or week and a proposed technology to be used in the productive system. The selection of a process, as suggested in Chapter 2, is a strategic decision. It helps determine—along with choices of product characteristics and market segments—the long-range competitive position or strategy of your company. Your choice of a process will affect variable and fixed costs of production and the future flexibility of the company. Some production processes are dedicated to one product and cannot be shifted to different items, for example, while others are restricted to one rate and cannot be changed to expand or reduce production volume.

The process decision is an important one for the beginning firm. This is why we previously recommended that new company founders examine a range of alternative processes and related products in a product-process matrix. Now you must select one which is adapted to your proposed product line, expected sales volume, and desired cost position. In making this selection, there are predictable problems you should anticipate.

PROCESS CAPACITY

Capacity is an easy-to-grasp concept—it refers to the amount of materials, goods, or services which can be produced by physical facilities and assigned workers in a production process over a specified period of time—but it can be difficult to measure. The capacity of a continuous (production line type) process that manufactures homogeneous products (such as shirts, appliances, or electronic memory chips) can be measured in units of output per hour. The capacity of an intermittent (job shop type) process that produces heterogeneous products (such as computer software, repair services, or educational programs) can only be measured by units of input available for processing.

A software consulting firm, for example, may employ three engineers and five programmers. Their combined total input is 320 hours of work activity per week. This available time might be applied to one large project or ten routine assignments; neither output figure would truly reflect the capacity of the firm.

Capacity is frequently more difficult to measure than you might imagine. It often can only be approximated in the process decision of the beginning firm.

PROCESS TECHNOLOGY

Technology presents problems which are almost the exact opposite of capacity: It is an easy factor to measure but a nearly impossible-to-define concept. Technology is the application of scientific theories to commercial products or processes. This may seem simple enough, but there is such a wide range of theories in use in different scientific fields and considerable variation in the levels of application originating from any one field. It becomes a challenge to succinctly describe the technology of a production process. The results of a particular process technology, however, can be readily measured and compared for alternative processes. Scales of measurement are: variable and fixed costs per unit of output.

Technology is frequently difficult to define. But costs can be roughly computed and compared for different technologies before making a process decision in a beginning firm.

OPERATIONAL ANALYSIS

Once your product design has been set (following standardization and simplification of components) and a production process has been selected (with a given capacity and technology), the next step in production planning is operational analysis. When this is done, you will have specified the series of operations necessary to produce your material, service, or good.

In a typical manufacturing company, engineering drawings detail the specifications for each part and bills of material list and classify the number of parts in each assembly. Operational analysis translates these technical requirements into routing slips which show steps needed to manufacture each part and put together each assembly. The same type of analysis should be performed for raw material processing or personal services preparation, although engineering drawings and bills of material for such "products" are usually lacking.

Operational analysis, whether for raw materials, personal services, or manufactured goods, is a detailed but straightforward process. Picture in your mind the series of separate steps needed to produce each part. Then list the parts needed for final assembly. This series of steps and list of parts is often shown graphically, as illustrated in Figure 4-2. Two very simple processes were selected: preparing coal for shipment and hamburger sandwiches for sale.

For some manufactured products there are so many operations that routing sheets become many pages long. Occasionally the paths of

FIGURE 4-2 Examples of simple process operations.

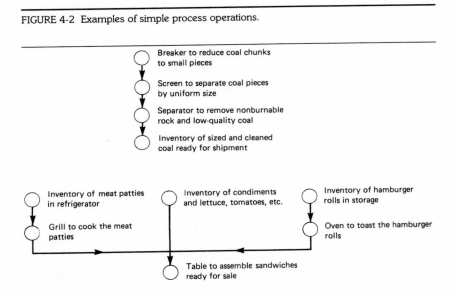

parts through a production process are so complex they cannot be charted on paper, but must be mathematically modeled with a computer. Despite such complexity, the principles of operational analysis remain the same. First identify a series of activities needed to create each part. Then specify all stages of assembly.

EQUIPMENT SELECTION

Following operational analysis comes selection of physical equipment needed for operations and assembly. The nature of equipment, of course, differs for each production process. Primary considerations in the selection are

1. Total capacity, generally expressed in units of either input or output per hour
2. Fixed expenses, usually measured by the total amount of the original investment depreciated over the life of the equipment plus charges for interest, taxes, and so forth
3. Variable costs, which include labor, power, maintenance, and so on

Capacity and technology will have been determined by your earlier decision on a production process to be used. Equipment selection ordinarily is limited to choices among various makes and models. Here, two secondary considerations should be weighed.

1. **Degree of automation.** There has been a tendency in production management over the past 20 years to add automation and cut labor. The intended result is to reduce costs. Too often, an unintended result has been the generation of dull, repetitive jobs which are poorly performed by unmotivated employees.

    Today, the application of automation is oriented more toward dangerous or harmful working environments and to eliminate rather than simplify jobs. Examples include the use of robotics in paint spraying, lead melting, and car welding. As you select equipment, consider the probable impact of automated machinery upon employee job performance.
2. **Possibility of purchase.** All of the parts in a completed product need not be made in-house; some may be purchased externally. In

an established company, such "make-buy" decisions usually revolve around the internal (per unit) costs of production versus a quoted purchase price (provided there is adequate capacity in-house). Non-financial factors, including supply reliability and quality assurance, are also weighed.

For a beginning firm, the most important consideration may be the possibility of increasing output without increasing investment. At this stage in production planning, comparative make-buy costs can be roughly estimated. New company founders should carefully consider the possibility of external purchase.

OPERATIONAL SEQUENCE

Once process equipment has been selected, individual machines and assembly stations must be combined into a productive system. A "system" may be defined as a set of interrelated components designed to accomplish a specific function. Consequently, a productive system is a set of interrelated machines and workstations needed to produce a particular raw material, personal service, or manufactured good at a certain unit volume and known dollar cost.

Interrelationships are the key to system effectiveness. In a productive system, they are represented by the flow of material. Two basic patterns of material flow are possible: continuous (line production) and intermittent (job-shop production); there are also various blends of these two extremes.

CONTINUOUS PROCESSING

Continuous processing moves material among individual machines and assembly stations in a fixed sequence. Often, the material is carried by conveyor belt past successive work areas; the sequence cannot be changed without complete redesign of the system.

Continuous production methods are usually considered best for products of medium- to high-volume and standardized designs. Some variation in product design is possible, but changes cannot be basic or extensive. Common examples of continuous processing are assembly lines for automobiles, appliances, and packaged foods. The method also is applicable in chemical plants and oil refineries. In fact, most basic manufacturing processes are continuous because they yield low cost at high volume.

The major problem with continuous production lies in difficulties of balancing the work load among individual machines and assembly stations. Each machine and station typically has a different capacity in units per hour. Since equipment is tied together in a continuous process chain, the output of an entire line is limited to the speed of the slowest link.

In "line balancing" additional machines or stations are added to share the load or operations are subdivided to reduce the work. The intent is to design the system with all machines and stations performing assignments accomplished at complementary time intervals. Line balancing techniques establish operation times for separate portions of each task and prescribe fixed sequences reflecting the technical constraints which limit each job. Individual tasks and jobs are then mathematically combined to find a balanced pattern.

Because of the huge number of alternatives available in many manufacturing systems, line balancing solutions seldom are optimal, but they are normally acceptable. You may want to hire professional help to balance an assembly line, or you can do it by trial and error during the first few months of operation.

INTERMITTENT PROCESSING

Intermittent processing moves material among individual machines and assembly stations in a variable sequence. Usually equipment is organized by department with all machines of a particular type located in one area. The material often is moved between departments by hand rather than by conveyor belt; sequences can be easily changed. Intermittent production is considered best for products of medium- to low-volume and nonstandardized designs.

Common examples of intermittent processing are various kinds of contract manufacturers—machine shops, tool and die makers, or short-run printers. They accomplish many diverse jobs requested by their customers. Other examples include such services as medical clinics, educational programs, and governmental agencies. Most service organizations use intermittent processes because they accommodate different products and permit variations in output.

The major problem with intermittent production is difficulty in scheduling work assignments for individual machines and assembly stations. Since each product normally has a different design, each requires a different set of operations. "Job-shop scheduling" assigns specific operations to individual machines and assembly stations according to the current backlog of orders and the processing costs at each work place. The intent is to manage the system to finish products on the agreed date at the lowest possible cost. Scheduling solution techniques can be visual (through the use of Gantt charts) or mathematical (through the use of linear programming).

Again, because of the large number of possible alternatives job-shop scheduling solutions are rarely optimal, but they are usually acceptable. It may be advisable to get professional help to set up visual charts and mathematical models, or you can rely on trial and error solutions over time.

MACHINE LOCATION

Operational analysis establishes a series of operations to be performed on each part and the number of parts required for each assembly. Machine selection chooses the physical equipment needed for operations and assembly at an estimated capacity level and expected unit cost. Operational sequencing combines individual machines and assembly stations into a productive system of interrelated work places fed by a continuous or intermittant flow of material.

The remaining step in the design of physical facilities is plant floor layout. For the beginning firm, processing equipment and workstations ordinarily must be positioned within the walls of an available building. There are two basic considerations in plant layout.

1. **Material transport.** Machines and workstations are interrelated by material flow, and a natural tendancy among those inexperienced in the layout of a new productive system is to minimize distances over which parts must be moved. Close proximity of related work places may be valuable in heavy manufacturing, but few start-up

firms need to be overly concerned about it. The transport of most materials and parts is relatively simple—whether by conveyor belt, forklift, or hand. You should place higher priority on human factors.

2. **Human factors.** Machines and workstations in a productive system are manned by people. Through plant layout it is possible to substantially improve work environments (noise, heat, light, etc.) and worker attitudes (opportunities for interaction, cooperation, etc.).

New company founders should consider the human factors of job design, job standards, group norms, and group standards (described in the following sections) before deciding on final placement of machines and workstations. One advantage enjoyed by new companies is a work force uncontaminated by past practices and policies. Potentially positive attitudes can be encouraged by the layout of the productive system.

PHYSICAL FACILITIES

Physical facilities result from the implementation of decisions on operational analysis, equipment selection, operational sequencing, and plant layout: This is the classical approach to plant or office design. Many start-up ventures do not follow the approach in its entirety.

Many more successful companies have begun in basements, garages, and barns with used and remodeled machinery, than in modern buildings with new equipment. Customers often prefer to do business with young firms in older facilities because they feel they are not helping to pay high overhead associated with modern buildings and equipment. Most financial professionals—both commercial bankers and venture capitalists—share this attitude. They believe managers of a growing firm should put their limited resources into current working capital rather than long-term fixed assets.

There are exceptions to the rule, of course. For many high-technology ventures, used equipment is not available. Founders of all high-growth companies, however, should carefully consider possibilities of purchasing externally produced parts, buying remodeled machinery, and leasing low-cost building space at the start.

JOB DESIGN

A productive system has been defined as a set of interrelated machines and assembly stations designed to produce a particular raw material, personal service, or manufactured good at a certain unit volume and expected dollar cost. This definition is precise and accurate, but it is also lifeless. It fails to mention people.

People are an integral part of productive systems of both continuous and intermittent types. Jobs must be designed for these people so their work can be performed without being overly tiring, frustrating, or irritating.

Work can be tiring if it demands muscular effort (as in logging or loading freight cars), manual dexterity (as in typing or assembling small parts), or logical decision-making (as in accounting or writing computer programs). Work can be frustrating if it cannot be completed in a reasonable time period (as in attempting to assemble parts without the right tolerances or trying to disassemble parts without the right tools). Work can be irritating if it has to be performed in a stressful setting with inadequate heat or light or under noxious conditions with excessive dust or noise. Job design attempts to improve all of these factors while maintaining or raising performance levels. The process of job design can be divided into three steps: determination of work content, recommendations for work methods, and design of the work environment.

1. **Work content** is not independently designed; it is a direct result of prior decisions on product design and process method. If the founders of a fast-food restaurant, for example, have decided to offer a sandwich made with a quarter-pound frozen meat patty and planned to cook those patties in a gas-fired grill with a moving conveyor, then the work content is set.

   Someone will have to separate the patties and place them on the conveyor. Another worker must remove cooked patties from the conveyor and assemble the sandwich. Work content is what a worker must do to make the system operate. This may be studied by breaking down each required activity into the motions a typical worker will make in performing the job.

2. **Work methods** are consciously designed; they are the direct results of efforts to improve performance of work content through

changes in work-place layout or process machine controls. Once again using our fast-food restaurant example, work-methods design might provide a table at a comfortable height to hold the meat patties as they are being placed on the conveyor. It might also consider ways to thaw the patties for easy separation.

Work methods are what a worker should do to make the system operate simply and safely. They may be studied by breaking down each improved activity into the motions of an efficient worker performing the job.

3. **Work environment** is the setting in which work methods are performed to accomplish work content. Design considerations include temperature, humidity, noise, lighting, smoke, fumes, and dust, all conditions which can irritate or harm workers and restrict the output.

The most harmful working conditions have been outlawed by state and federal legislation such as the U.S. Occupational Safety and Health Act of 1967. Beyond compliance with the law, there are many opportunities, particularly in nonindustrial settings, to raise productivity and increase quality by improving individual work environments.

JOB STANDARDS

A job standard refers to the amount of time it should take an average worker to perform a specific job (once optimal work methods have been developed and an improved work environment has been created). Job standards are used for production planning, scheduling, and control and for computing product cost and employee wage incentives. In other words, they help manage a productive system.

Job or time standards can be applied only to repetitive tasks in a factory, office, or service agency. The first step is to list required motions of the work content. These are, as previously suggested, what a worker should do to make the productive system operate simply and safely. They portray the actions of an efficient worker in performing the job. Time standards may be applied to these motions in one of two ways.

1. **Stopwatch analysis.** Select one or two representative workers who are experienced and trained in the work methods and who

work at a normal pace. Then time each of their motions with a stopwatch.

Numerous readings usually are obtained. Allowances are added for relief time, system delays, and worker fatigue. Then, the mean time and standard deviation are computed for each motion. The problem with stopwatch analysis, of course, lies in singling out a worker who will be accepted by his or her peers as representative and in defining a pace which can be assumed to be normal.

2. **Employee participation.** Ask a group of workers to develop their own standard times. Let them report the results to you.

Stopwatch studies are resented by many people, and they tend to be inaccurate because of pace changes inspired by this resentment. A start-up venture—with new employees—can often develop useful standards for production scheduling and cost control by relying on workers to reach consensus estimates of times required for performing repetitive tasks.

GROUP STRUCTURE

There is a new attitude toward worker involvement in the management of productive systems. It stems from the demonstrated efficiency of certain foreign systems and from the resulting competitive pressures on many domestic plants to increase productivity, reduce costs, and improve quality.

New approaches to labor-management cooperation cannot be explained fully in a single chapter, but new company founders should consider the importance of "group structures." Worker attitudes and employee motivations derive from relationships between people within a work group. These work groups, or group structures, operate formally or informally within every productive system.

Group structure often was neglected by managers in the past. Production management traditionally emphasized job specialization and job engineering and ignored group influences. It was believed there had to be a division of labor with work divided into specialized tasks, each of which required different operations and skills. It was expected that through continual repetition of tasks skill levels would increase and labor costs would come down. A festering problem, however, was that people (within specialized and engineered productive systems) worked individually at dull and repetitive tasks. They often had no opportunity to cooperate or interact with each other. Specialization destroyed group structure; with this structure went positive group norms for improved productivity and quality.

New approaches to production management emphasize job enrichment and work redesign to rebuild group structure. It is now generally believed there should be opportunities for achievement, responsibility, and recognition within each work group. These three attitudinal factors (and their contributing elements) should be defined from the viewpoint of a person at work in the productive system.

1. Worker belief in *achievement* of an outcome. A person must feel he or she is assigned to important work. This attitude hinges on task variety (different types of work providing interest and challenge), task identity (one complete unit of work performed from beginning to end), and task significance (overall impact of the work, both inside and outside the company).
2. Worker belief in *responsibility* for an outcome. A person has to feel he or she is personally responsible for performing the work. This attitude depends upon task identity (one complete unit of work) and task autonomy (discretion in planning and carrying out the work).
3. Worker belief in *recognition* of an outcome. A person must feel he or she is recognized for work performance. This attitude is instilled by task identity (one complete unit of work) and task feedback (direct evaluation of work performance).

People differ in their responses to job enrichment and work redesign depending upon their knowledge, skill, and ability to perform the tasks and upon their needs for task variety, task identity, task significance, and so on. Not everyone likes the personal results of job significance, responsibility, and recognition.

Productive systems differ in their potential for job enrichment and work redesign depending upon their technological requirements (some job activities, dictated by machine operations, cannot be changed), personnel restrictions (some job assignments, the result of union-management negotiations, cannot be changed), and organizational constraints (some job characteristics, because of existing control systems, accounting methods, or professional obligations, cannot be changed). Not all productive systems permit work roles rich in job significance, responsibility, and recognition.

GROUP NORMS

If you do change work design to add significance, responsibility, and recognition to each and every job, generally the result is that the productive system becomes organized around groups rather than around individuals.

Particular tasks—such as soldering twelve wires to the chassis of a television set as it moves along an assembly line—are often difficult to infuse with significance. Group activities—such as assemblying an entire set—may become more significant if the group is made responsible for quality and given recognition for output. For this reason, work redesign normally focuses on groups rather than individuals.

Groups must be organized to perform the work content dictated by product design and process methods. But, within the group, work content typically is broken into individual portions and then recombined according to agreed upon patterns. Thus, the most efficient means of performing the work (the work method) may change and job standards (expected time required to perform the work) may be dispensed with.

One work redesign concept, for example, might assign responsibility for assembling television sets to a group, allowing group members to decide on the most efficient means of soldering twelve wires to the chassis. Time standards for this task would become meaningless; the important issue would be group productivity in assembling television sets, not the number of wires soldered. Group norms, enforced by peer pressure, tend to ensure that the person soldering wires works with the same effort and attention as other members of the group assigned to different portions of the total task.

Five rules must be considered when forming groups to perform the work content in a productive system. These rules are intended to define activities which group members will consider significant and to establish outcomes for which members will be willing to accept responsibility and pleased to receive recognition.

1. **Combine activities** from the work content to produce a larger and more interesting "module" of work. This tends to add task variety and improve task identity.

   Find a natural stopping place in the productive system at which the work module includes a complete set of activities and results in a finished unit which can be measured for productivity and examined for quality. This method is simple for the assembly of small products such as television sets or the quick delivery of services such as fast-foods, but it is difficult to apply to more complex goods such as automobiles or more professional services such as nursing care. The combination of activities into work modules often is a challenging but critical first step in job enrichment and group formation.

2. **Establish natural affiliations** for each work module by emphasizing task identity and increasing task significance and by setting up a recognized product or market base for each group.

   In a manufacturing process, the natural affiliation will be with the product type; each group should work on a given product or a subassembly of that product. In a service process, the natural affiliation will be with the market segment; each group should be identified by geographic territory (all appliance repairs in the northwest section of the city), by customer type (all typewriter repairs for law firms), or by organizational unit (all cost accounting for the company's typewriter manufacturing division).

3. **Form client relationships** for each work module. If there is a recognized base by product line or market segment for each work module, it becomes possible to set up client relationships for group members assigned to each module.

   Client relationships provide clear task identity, more task significance, and quicker task feedback. A group assigned responsibility for the repair of all typewriters in law firms within a given city, for example, may also be designated to administer all contacts with these law firms. Group members would respond to requests for prompt service and hear complaints about poor service. This is client relationship, the direct communication between the group responsible for producing a product or service and the people who receive that product or service.

   All clients are not necessarily external customers. For a cost accounting group, the client might be people in a manufacturing division of the same company. Communications between that division and the accounting group would be direct, explicit, and personal.

4. **Encourage internal scheduling** for activities in each work module. Once a natural affiliation has been established for each group and direct communication opened between group members and clients, then it is possible to permit group members to respond independently to demands for service.

   To continue the example of the typewriter repair group responsible for services to law firms within a particular city, group members would also be given responsibility for scheduling their own activities. In self-managing work groups, members are expected to be willing to work overtime or undertime to adjust their capacity to client needs.

5. **Arrange internal controls** for activities in each work module. After the establishment of a natural affiliation and direct communications between group members and clients in an affiliated base, arrange for each group to independently review and evaluate its own service.

   One reason for setting up group-client relationships is to permit direct and prompt feedback. Such feedback cannot be ignored; it must be discussed and corrective action taken. In self-managing work groups, individual members are expected to be both willing critics and supporters of other members and ready to change group standards to meet clients needs.

Self-managing work groups—with assigned modules, established affiliations, direct communications, internal scheduling, and internal controls—are small productive systems in which human elements take precedence over technical factors. These work groups can be very effective, but they are not appropriate in all situations. As previously suggested, the potential for work redesign is dependent upon technological requirements, personnel restrictions, and organizational constraints.

Where conditions are appropriate, self-managing work groups offer the possibility of much greater effort being applied to assigned tasks. This is never a certainty. Not all self-managing work groups are successful, and not all work redesign projects result in higher labor productivity and better output quality. Factors increasing the probability of success appear to be clarity of group tasks, composition of group membership, and development of group norms.

Group norms refer to standards of behavior accepted by members of the group. When these standards reinforce central management objectives of raising labor productivity, increasing output quality, and making smooth decision processes for scheduling and control, self-managing work groups can prove dramatically successful.

New company founders may determine the clarity of group tasks and influence the composition of group memberships, but they cannot control the development of group norms. You should recognize that group norms *will develop* no matter what you do—either formally (within a self-managing work group) or informally (through socializing among workers). Those norms (both formal and informal) will influence the output volume, unit costs, and quality standards of the productive system.

INTRODUCTION TO QUANTITATIVE METHODS

The capacity for both continuous and intermittent processing systems is normally computed at an assumed, stable level of demand—with all machines and assembly stations performing at an optimum pace. In the real world, demand is seldom stable. It varies over time (stage of the business cycle, season of the year, day of the week). It also varies by product or service type, with a total demand level (meals in a fast-food restaurant for example) and a component level for individual products and services (hamburgers versus chicken sandwiches).

Worker performance varies according to individual attitudes and abilities (the number of chicken sandwiches prepared per hour by employee A versus employee B). The performance of machinery also fluctuates depending upon maintenance and repair requirements.

The actual capacity of a productive system's physical facilities differs from the designed capacity according to the level and type of demand and the performance effort. Quantitative methods for production planning, scheduling, and control have been developed to adjust system output in response to these variations and to achieve optimal facilities utilization at minimal cost.

PRODUCTION PLANNING METHODS

Production planning adjusts the designed capacity of physical facilities to meet variations in total, or "aggregate," demand, which may vary over time. Adjustments can be made in the aggregate capacity of the system by making changes in employment level, employment hours, finished inventory, or external purchases.

1. **Changes in employment level.** People can be added to the existing productive system on a single shift by subdividing operations and rebalancing the system. More people may be added on a second or third shift, although this will also require increased administration, supervision, and maintenance. Additional costs are associated with hiring and training new employees to boost production or with the discharge and compensation of persons to decrease production. Changes in employment level can become very expensive.

2. **Changes in employment hours.** Existing employees can be asked to work overtime (48 hours per week) or undertime (32 hours). Changes greater than plus or minus 8 hours are generally considered to cause fatigue or harm morale. Thus, this method of capacity adjustment is limited to approximately plus or minus 20 percent. Additional costs associated with overtime or undertime are usually much greater than 20 percent.

3. **Changes in finished inventory.** Inventory build-up can be planned in anticipation of a sales surge, or an order backlog can be tolerated as a result of an unexpected sales increase. An order backlog is a negative inventory position; additional costs arise from lost contributions to revenue and irritated customers. An inventory buildup is, of course, positive; extra costs accrue from interest charges on working capital, storage and handling expenses, and possibly from obsolescence or spoilage. Changes in inventory level—both positive and negative—generally are associated with changes in lengths of production runs which, in turn, affect setup and reorder costs. Mathematical models may be applied to relate increases or decreases in these costs to changes in inventory level.

4. **Changes in external purchases.** Make-buy decisions computed at one level of capacity utilization may change with variations in that level. External purchases of parts and subassemblies can increase the actual capacity of existing facilities by reassigning the remaining

operations and rebalancing the system, but there are additional purchase costs and lost margins associated with this alternative.

In a brief explanation of productive system design for start-up ventures, it is not possible to describe all the quantitative techniques applicable to production planning. The objective of each of these techniques is to minimize total costs of meeting a changed aggregate level of demand—within the limitations of an existing physical facility. This objective can be realized by examining variables for a single time period (a single-stage model) or for sequential time periods (a multiple-stage model).

Multiple-stage models are more realistic because changes in one time period obviously change conditions in succeeding periods. Multiple-stage models also are mathematically more complex. For those interested in exploring the topic further, two mathematical techniques most often used in multiple-stage production planning are called "quadratic programming" and "computer simulation."

PRODUCTION SCHEDULING METHODS

Production scheduling adjusts the designed capacity of physical facilities to meet variations in demand for individual products or services. This activity addresses component rather than aggregate demand, one product or service versus another. Component demand also varies over time.

Adjustments can be made in the component capacity of a continuous (line) productive system by changeover of the line. This creates a host of attendant problems: rebalancing operations and retraining workers.

Adjustments can be made in the component capacity of an intermittent (job shop) productive system by making changes in product mix, facility assignments, or order priorities.

1. **Changes in product mix.** It is possible to respond to component demand changes in an intermittent processing system by changing the product mix; more of the product or service demanded can be produced. This is ordinarily a simple adjustment unless the productive system is operating at full capacity. Then it becomes necessary

to produce less of another product or service, and therefore the optimal product mix must be considered.

If the capacity limit of the system has been reached, the optimal product mix will generate the maximum contribution (sales revenues less fixed and variable costs) possible from current product demands and existing physical facilities. Usually, each product or service generates a different contribution per unit and involves different time requirements at each process machine or assembly station. For those interested, the general allocation method of linear programming is most often used to select an optimal mix of products; it identifies specific quantities of each product type which will yield the highest overall contribution and most fully utilize existing facilities.

2. **Changes in facilities assignment.** It is possible to respond to component demand changes in an intermittent processing system by changing machine assignments; the product or service demanded can be routed to faster machines and assembly stations. This, again, is normally a simple adjustment as long as the system is not operating at full capacity.

   At full capacity, the optimal facility assignment has to be considered. It may be mathematically determined by using the assignment method of linear programming or through computer simulation.

3. **Changes in order priorities.** It is also possible to respond to component demand changes in an intermittent processing system by changing order priorities; production of the product or service demanded can be given precedence. Within the productive system, there is generally an in-process inventory of partially completed products waiting at each machine and assembly station. Depending upon the priority at which these waiting components are processed, the total time for completion of each of the goods and services produced by the productive system may be varied. Some can be made to go through the system very quickly and others at a more leisurely pace. The priority ranking method established at each machine and assembly station can be as simple as first come, first served, or it can be slightly more complex, based upon shortest remaining processing time or earliest due date. Overall effects of changes in order priorities may be studied through computer simulation.

PRODUCTION CONTROL METHODS

Production control adjusts the output of the productive system for variations in individual worker or machine performance. Production supervisors record performance criteria (physical units, operational times, and quality tolerances) and compare measurements with accepted standards. These standards come from time studies (for the workers) and engineering designs (for the machines). They are charted against levels of products and services—the output of the system.

1. **Worker control.** Each person's working performance within a productive system can be measured against time and quality standards, employing "variance analysis" to uncover reasons for deviations from standards. Differences between standard and actual performance can be caused by a worker's lack of effort or attention or by problems arising elsewhere in the system such as slow delivery of needed parts or poor tolerances in prior operations. Because wage incentives and bonus payments often are based upon worker performance, new company founders should recognize all the possible causes of performance variations.

2. **Machine control.** Each machine's performance within a productive system also can be measured against time and quality standards, usually by using statistical sampling methods. Sample measurements may be taken at regular intervals and variations from standard performance noted.

   Corrections in machine performance may be made without concern for individual attitudes or group norms except in those situations in which the worker and the machine are interdependent. Such instances are not uncommon. They require special methods to separate the efforts of the worker from the problems of the machine and to evaluate the contributions of each to productivity and quality measures of performance.

3. **Output control.** The performance of the complete productive system may be gauged by making periodic comparisons of output (in physical units), operational times, and quality tolerances. Remember, however, that it is difficult to define output capacities for intermittent processing systems (because of the lack of homogeneous products), and it is difficult to establish operational times and qual-

ity tolerances for services (because of the lack of measureable dimensions). New company founders should make an effort to measure output, not only to ensure high performance but also to fairly reward those responsible for it.

Development of a productive system for a new company is a complex task. You can work out such a system by thinking through each of its components in a logical sequence. This complete sequence, shown graphically in Figure 4-1, stresses the relationships among various production management components.

CHAPTER FIVE
FINANCIAL
PLANNING

The financial plan for a start-up venture should be based upon marketing and production plans prepared earlier by company founders. Your chosen product-market position and the marketing plan adapted to it will determine your new company's anticipated sales revenues, marketing expenses, and the funds needed to support finished goods inventory and finance customer account receivable. Your product-process position and productive system design, likewise, will determine your expected output volume, unit costs, and the investments necessary for plant and equipment. Together these prior decisions on marketing and production set the financial requirements for the firm. Financial planning recognizes these requirements, forecasts the amounts, investigates the sources, computes the costs, and arranges the availability of financing.

Financial planning is difficult but not impossible for new company founders to learn. We will illustrate the planning process for a hypothetical firm, assuming the new company has been in existence for 3 or more years. This vantage point was selected because high-growth companies often do start slowly, almost informally, before financial plans are completed. And it is easier to first explain financial forecasting through a discussion of ratio and cost analysis for an existing firm than it is to start with a description of how to forecast financial needs through "pro forma statements" and "cash flow budgets" for an entirely new company.

Pro forma statements are balance sheets and income statements projected for specific future periods. Cash flow budgets itemize the expected sources and uses of funds over these specific future periods. Together the pro forma statements and cash flow budgets indicate needs for external financing from bank loans, personal and family

FIGURE 5-1 Relationships among components of financial planning.

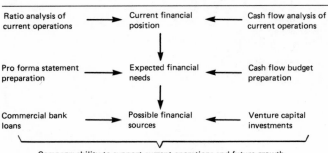

Company ability to support current operations and future growth

investments, and venture capital. Most high-growth firms use a mixture of these external financing sources.

To help you arrange external financing, we will discuss, in turn, analysis of a firm's current financial position, projection of future financial needs, means of applying for bank loans, and methods of requesting venture capital. This is complete financial planning—because it brings the uses and sources of funds into the process. Financial planning of this magnitude is shown graphically in Figure 5-1.

The objective of financial planning is to obtain funds needed to support the planned growth of your company and to adjust your growth plan to the availability of funds. Money is not automatically supplied to small or beginning firms. Shortages of funds often limit the scope of a marketing plan or the size of a productive system. New company founders have to apply limited amounts of money to the most important uses and gradually build a reputation for reliability and performance among the prime sources of additional money: commercial banks and venture capitalists.

A reputation for reliability and performance requires detailed financial planning—and adherence to those plans. This chapter explains each of the elements of a detailed financial plan; you must use them to develop realistic goals and objectives for your beginning firm.

RATIO ANALYSIS

Financial planning relies heavily on "ratio analysis" of existing operations. These ratios, which relate two or more categories of financial data, can be used to judge past performance and the current position of the firm and to forecast future needs. Historical ratios are particularly useful because they can be compared across time periods to establish trends and between your company's record and industry averages to identify problems. Six types of financial ratios are commonly computed from balance sheet and income statement data.

1. **Liquidity ratios** show the firm's ability to meet short-term debts. They are used to indicate *credit strength* or financial risk. Commonly used liquidity ratios include the current ratio and the acid-test ratio.

$$\text{Current ratio} = \frac{\text{current asset}}{\text{current liabilities}}$$

$$\text{Acid-test ratio} = \frac{\text{current assets} - \text{inventory}}{\text{current liabilities}}$$

2. **Profitability ratios** show the company's profitability in relation to either sales or investment. They are used to indicate the *operational efficiency* of the firm. Commonly used profitability ratios include return on sales, return on assets, and return on equity.

$$\text{Return on sales} = \frac{\text{profits after tax}}{\text{total sales}}$$

$$\text{Return on assets} = \frac{\text{profits after tax}}{\text{total assets}}$$

$$\text{Return on equity} = \frac{\text{profits after tax}}{\text{total equity (assets} - \text{debt)}}$$

3. **Utilization ratios** show the firm's ability to manage short-term assets. They are used to indicate the *financial efficiency* of the company. Commonly used utilization ratios include receivables in days, inventory in days, and payables in days.

$$\text{Receivables in days} = \frac{\text{accounts receivable}}{\text{annual sales} \div 360 \text{ days}}$$

$$\text{Inventory in days} = \frac{\text{total inventory}}{\text{annual cost of goods sold} \div 360 \text{ days}}$$

$$\text{Payables in days} = \frac{\text{accounts payable}}{\text{annual purchases} \div 360 \text{ days}}$$

4. **Debt ratios** show the proportion of debt in the company's capital structure. They are used to indicate the *credit strength* or financial

risk of the firm. Commonly used debt ratios include the debt to equity ratio and the long-term debt percentage.

$$\text{Debt to equity ratio} = \frac{\text{total debt (current liabilities + long-term debt)}}{\text{total equity (assets − debt)}}$$

$$\text{Long-term debt percentage} = \frac{\text{long-term debt}}{\text{total capitalization (assets − current liabilities)}}$$

5. **Coverage ratios** show the firm's ability to meet fixed financial charges of long-term debt in the capital structure. They are also used to indicate the *credit strength* or financial risk of the company. Commonly used coverage ratios include number of times debt interest is earned, and number of times debt payments (both interest and principle) are earned.

$$\text{Debt interest earned} = \frac{\text{company profits before interest and tax}}{\text{annual debt interest payments}}$$

$$\text{Debt payments earned} = \frac{\text{company profits before interest and tax}}{\text{annual debt (interest and principle) payments}}$$

6. **Expense ratios** show the company's various expense categories in relation to sales. They are used to compare the firm's recent performance with past time periods and with industry averages. Expense ratios are commonly calculated for all major expense categories such as material cost, labor cost, selling expense, and professional (legal and accounting) services.

$$\text{Expense ratio} = \frac{\text{expense category}}{\text{annual sales}}$$

To illustrate the use of ratio analysis, consider sample financial data from a hypothetical small company (see Figures 5-2 and 5-3) with sales of $211,420 and profits after tax of $2040, as detailed in the income statement and balance sheet. Assume this company was formed 4 years ago to make electronic test instruments—perhaps a high-quality frequency counter and frequency synthesizer. The company has not grown as rapidly as expected. Now its founders are beginning to think about acquiring additional capital needed to expand the sales effort. Your assignment is to develop a financial plan for the firm. You start with ratio analysis.

FIGURE 5-2 Sample income statement.

	Expense dollars	Expense ratios
	XYZ Electronics, Inc. **Income Statement** **Last Year**	
Sales	$211,420	100.0%
Material cost	59,410	28.1%
Labor cost	69,980	33.1%
Shop supervision	12,050	5.7%
Shop overhead	17,130	8.1%
Total manufacturing costs	158,570	75.0%
Gross margin	52,850	25.0%
Personal selling	7,820	3.7%
Advertising	1,910	0.9%
Total marketing expenses	9,730	4.6%
Executive and staff salaries	22,190	10.5%
Interest expense	7,710	3.7%
Telephone expense	2,650	1.2%
Professional services	3,070	1.4%
Office overhead	4,860	2.3%
Total administrative expenses	40,480	19.1%
Profits before tax	2,640	1.3%
Federal income tax (25%)	630	0.3%
Profits after tax	2,040	1.0%

You can prepare the various financial ratios for this company, as shown below, by using previously described computational rules upon the financial data given in the income statement and balance sheet.

$$\text{Current ratio} = \frac{\text{current assets}}{\text{current liabilities}} = \frac{\$78,720}{\$59,470} = 1.3 \text{ to } 1$$

$$\text{Acid-test ratio} = \frac{\text{current assets} - \text{inventory}}{\text{current liabilities}}$$

$$= \frac{\$78,720 - \$38,260}{\$59,470} = 0.7 \text{ to } 1$$

FIGURE 5-3 Sample balance sheet.

XYZ Electronics, Inc.
Balance Sheet
Last Year

Assets		Liabilities	
Cash	$ 2,150	Accrued salaries & wages	$ 4,850
Accounts receivable	36,310	Accounts payable	17,250
Inventory	38,260	Withholding taxes due	1,860
Prepaid expenses	2,000	Bank loan—due 1 year	25,000
Current assets	78,720	Eqpt. fin.—due 1 year	10,510
		Current liabilities	59,470
Equipment	33,200	Long-term debt—eqpt.	10,000
Less depreciation	6,900	Long-term debt—mort.	33,500
Net equipment	26,300	Total long-term debt	43,500
Building	52,000	Common stock	22,000
Less depreciation	9,600	Retained earnings	22,450
Net property	42,400	Total owners equity	44,450
Total assets	$147,420	Total liabilities/equity	$147,420

$$\text{Return on sales} = \frac{\text{profits after tax}}{\text{total sales}} = \frac{\$2040}{\$211,420} = 1.0\%$$

$$\text{Return on assets} = \frac{\text{profits after tax}}{\text{total assets}} = \frac{\$2040}{\$147,420} = 1.4\%$$

$$\text{Return on equity} = \frac{\text{profits after tax}}{\text{total equity}} = \frac{\$2040}{\$44,450} = 4.6\%$$

$$\text{Accounts receivables in days} = \frac{\text{accounts receivable}}{\text{annual sales} \div 360}$$

$$= \frac{\$36,310}{\$211,420 \div 360} = 62 \text{ days}$$

$$\text{Inventory in days} = \frac{\text{inventory}}{\text{cost goods sold} \div 360}$$

$$= \frac{\$38,260}{\$158,570 \div 360} = 87 \text{ days}$$

$$\text{Accounts payable in days} = \frac{\text{accounts payable}}{\text{purchases} \div 360}$$

$$= \frac{\$17,250}{(\$59,410 + \$17,130) \div 360} = 81$$

$$\text{Debt to equity ratio} = \frac{\text{total debt}}{\text{total equity}}$$

$$= \frac{\$59,470 + \$43,500}{\$44,450} = 2.3 \text{ to } 1$$

$$\text{Long-term debt percentage} = \frac{\text{long-term debt}}{\text{total capitalization}}$$

$$= \frac{\$43,500}{\$43,500 + \$44,450} = 49.5\%$$

$$\text{Debt interest earned} = \frac{\text{profits before interest and tax}}{\text{annual debt payments}}$$

$$= \frac{\$7710 + \$2640}{\$7710} = 1.35$$

Financial ratios for a single year are interesting; these same ratios, compared to prior years or with industry averages, are vital to achieving an understanding of the operations and problems of a firm. Consider data on the same small company described previously, this time with financial reports (income statements and balance sheets) for 3 prior years as shown in Figures 5-4 and 5-5.

By quickly examining these basic, historical financial reports, it is immediately apparent that the company's profits are declining sharply. It is not exactly clear why this is happening nor what effect these declining profits may have had upon the credit strength or financial risk of the firm. A comparison of financial ratios—computed from this accounting data over the past 3 years—points up some important trends. A comparison of these trends to industry averages helps to identify operating problems and to understand there is a need for major financial changes (see Figure 5-6).

This complete ratio analysis suggests XYZ Electronics, Inc., has invested more than its company founders probably should have spent for fixed assets (productive equipment and a new building) in anticipation of an industry-wide sales revenue increase. Unfortunately, the company did not participate in the general sales increase, perhaps because of a low-scale marketing effort. Company founders are now faced with de-

FIGURE 5-4 Historical income statement.

	XYZ Electronics, Inc. Income Statement		
	3 Years Ago	2 Years Ago	Last Year
Sales revenues	$191,930	$207,410	$211,420
Material cost	53,360	56,830	59,410
Labor cost	56,620	65,540	69,980
Shop supervision	13,050	13,890	12,050
Shop overhead	11,700	16,180	17,130
Total manufacturing costs	134,730	152,440	158,750
Gross margin	57,200	54,970	52,850
Personal selling expenses	11,130	8,090	7,820
Advertising	2,110	1,240	1,910
Total marketing expenses	13,240	9,330	9,730
Executive and staff salaries	19,450	21,470	22,190
Interest expenses	4,090	7,540	7,710
Telephone expenses	2,480	2,690	2,650
Professional services	3,630	3,520	3,070
Office overhead	3,250	4,570	4,860
Total administrative expenses	32,900	39,790	40,480
Profits before tax	11,060	5,850	2,640
Federal income tax	2,880	1,450	630
Profits after tax	8,180	4,400	2,010

teriorating profits, brought about by increased depreciation charges in the shop overhead category and by additional interest costs in the administrative expenses category.

Labor costs also seem high, perhaps brought about by excess hiring for the anticipated production expansion; executive and staff salaries exceed the industry average. The worsening operating position of the company is reflected by poor current returns on sales, assets, and equity. The deteriorating financial condition of the firm is marked by low current and acid-test ratios, extension of the accounts payable, and a decline in debt interest earned.

FIGURE 5-5 Historical balance sheet.

XYZ Electronics Inc.
Balance Sheet

Assets

	3 Years Ago	2 Years Ago	Last Year
Cash	$ 3,060	$ 1,910	$ 2,150
Accounts receivable	21,940	38,170	36,310
Inventory	37,800	39,200	38,260
Prepaid expenses	1,410	1,770	2,000
Total current assets	64,210	71,050	78,720
Equipment account	18,670	23,440	33,200
Depreciation reserve	− 3,480	− 4,410	− 6,900
New equipment account	15,190	19,030	26,300
Building and land	24,130	52,000	52,000
Depreciation reserve	− 4,820	− 7,010	− 9,600
Net property account	19,310	44,990	42,400
Total current and fixed assets	98,710	135,070	147,420

Liabilities

	3 Years Ago	2 Years Ago	Last Year
Accrued salaries and wages	2,840	3,670	4,850
Accounts payable	5,780	9,730	17,250
Withholding taxes due	—	—	1,860
Bank loan—90 days note at 9%	19,000	23,000	25,000
Eqpt. loan—1 year contract 12%	6,440	9,750	10,510
Current liabilities	34,060	46,150	59,470
Eqpt. loan—2 year contract 12%	9,440	10,510	10,000
Bldg. loan—8 year mortgage 8%	18,550	38,000	35,500
Total long-term debt	27,990	48,510	43,500
Common stock	20,000	20,000	22,000
Retailed earnings	16,660	20,410	22,450
Total owners equity	36,660	40,410	44,450
Total liability and equity	98,710	135,070	147,420

FIGURE 5-6 Historical ratio analysis.

XYZ Electronics, Inc.				
	Company Ratios			Industry Averages
	3 Years Ago	2 Years Ago	Last Year	Last Year
Sales growth (1980 = 100)	106.1	115.3	117.5	167.7
Sales revenues	100.0%	100.0%	100.0%	100.0%
Material cost	27.8%	27.4%	28.1%	27.5%
Labor cost	29.5%	31.6%	33.1%	29.2%
Shop supervision	6.8%	6.7%	5.7%	6.8%
Shop overhead	6.1%	7.8%	8.5%	5.8%
Total manufacturing	70.2%	73.5%	75.0%	69.3%
Gross margin	29.8%	26.5%	25.0%	30.7%
Personal selling	5.8%	3.9%	3.7%	5.8%
Advertising	1.1%	0.6%	0.9%	1.6%
Total marketing	6.9%	4.5%	4.6%	7.4%
Executive and staff salaries	10.1%	10.4%	10.5%	9.0%
Interest expense	2.1%	3.6%	3.7%	2.0%
Telephone expense	1.3%	1.3%	1.3%	1.7%
Professional services	1.9%	1.7%	1.4%	1.1%
Office overhead	1.7%	2.2%	2.3%	2.2%
Total administrative	17.1%	19.2%	19.1%	16.2%
Profits before taxes	5.8%	2.8%	1.3%	7.1%
Federal income tax	1.5%	0.7%	0.3%	2.6%
Profit after taxes	4.3%	2.1%	1.0%	16.2%
Current ratio	1.88	1.54	1.32	2.10
Acid-test ratio	0.77	0.69	0.68	1.20
Return on sales	4.3%	2.1%	1.0%	4.5%
Return on assets	8.3%	3.3%	1.4%	9.2%
Return on equity	22.3%	11.1%	4.6%	17.5%
Accts. rec. in days	41.0	49.0	62.0	38.0
Inventory in days	101.0	93.0	87.0	67.0
Accts. pay. in days	32.0	48.0	81.0	22.0

	Company Ratios			Industry Averages
	3 Years Ago	2 Years Ago	Last Year	Last Year
Debt/equity ratio	1.7	2.3	2.3	1.3
Long-term debt	43.3%	54.6%	49.5%	28.7%
Debt interest earned	3.7	1.8	1.3	7.0
Current assets/total assets	65.0%	52.6%	53.3%	69.0%
Fixed assets/total assets	35.0%	47.4%	46.7%	31.0%

A bank probably would hesitate to advance additional funds to this company because of the desperate financial situation indicated by ratio analysis. Yet, if the founders decided to remedy operating problems by launching an intensive marketing campaign to increase sales, expenses of that campaign might be financed by reducing current assets invested in accounts receivable (62 days) and inventory (87 days), bringing these accounts closer to the industry averages. They might also consider selling excess machinery or renting out extra space in their new building. Financial ratio analysis does help in defining the problems of a firm and in designing solutions to those problems.

COST ANALYSIS

Cost analysis tends to mystify people with little training or experience in finance and accounting. There are many different classes, types, and styles of costs and alternative systems used to accumulate those costs and then to allocate them to products, functions, departments, and so forth.

Fortunately, it is not necessary to become a cost accountant to prepare pro forma statements and cash flow budgets. You need only understand the general nature of costs and their behavior relative to increases or decreases in production volume or sales revenues, then make reasonable and explicit assumptions about the future. The general nature of costs and their behavior relative to production or sales can be grasped by examining different classes, types, and styles of costs.

1. **Classes of costs.** The costs experienced within a business firm may be divided between those associated with the product or service produced and those tied to the general management of the company.

   "Cost of goods" sold is associated with the product or service; it usually includes material, labor, shop supervision, and manufacturing overhead. Manufacturing overhead includes power, heat, and light in the shop; taxes; interest and depreciation on the equipment and the portion of the building occupied by the shop; and the cost of small tools, cleaning supplies, and so on.

   "Gross margin" is the difference between sales revenues of the firm and the cost of goods sold. It represents the amount of money left over to cover selling and administrative costs and to make a contribution to company profits.

   "Selling and administrative expenses" are the costs associated with general management of the firm. It is traditional to use the term "expenses" when discussing selling and administrative costs "on the other side" of the gross margin. Selling and administrative expenses include personal selling, advertising and distribution costs, executive and staff salaries, interest expenses (except for the interest on machinery, equipment, and the portion of the building occupied by the shop), property taxes (except for taxes on production machinery and shop building space), telephone cost, professional services such as legal and accounting, and so forth.

2. **Types of costs.** The costs encountered by a business firm can be divided into variable, fixed, and semi-fixed types.

   "Variable costs" vary with production volume or sales level. Material and labor in the cost of goods sold usually are variable, and sales commissions in the selling and administrative expenses are variable.

   "Fixed costs" remain constant over a range of production rates or sales volumes. Shop supervision in the cost of goods sold usually is considered to be fixed. Executive salaries and professional services in the selling and administrative expenses are also fixed. Fixed does not mean without change under any circumstances; it merely suggests that within a given range of production rates or sales volumes costs remain relatively constant. If the production rate doubles, for example, costs of shop supervision eventually will rise, but probably not by an equal factor.

"Semi-fixed costs" vary in a discontinuous fashion, or in step-function, with changes in production or sales. They reflect a mixture of fixed and variable costs such as charges for electricity in manufacturing overhead. Some of the electricity is used for lighting which does not vary with production and some for power which does vary with production.

3. **Styles of costs.** The costs incurred within a business firm also may be classified as direct versus indirect and discretionary versus nondiscretionary.

"Direct costs" can be traced back to specific departments, products, or processes, while indirect costs cannot easily be identified with any "compartment" of the company and must be allocated. Allocation may be made on any reasonable basis. For example, XYZ Electronics, Inc., manufactures frequency counters and frequency synthesizers for electronic laboratory use. Material and labor costs of production are direct; they can easily be associated with one or another of the products. Shop supervision and manufacturing overhead are indirect; they must be allocated. Costs may be allocated to the different products according to a percentage of labor hours spent on each or to floor space used by each. Either method of allocation seems reasonable.

"Discretionary costs" are those which can easily be varied by management; nondiscretionary costs tend to be associated with some other factor in the financial plan and cannot easily be changed. Interest costs, for example, are associated with the size of a loan and cannot be varied by management except to the extent that loan size may be reduced or interest rate renegotiated. Personal selling expenses (salaries of sales people) and advertising expenses can be altered by a single management decision, although that decision will influence probable sales revenues and should be made with discretion.

Now that we have defined all the various costs, let us look again at the income statement for XYZ Electronics, Inc., embellished with classifications and predictions. (See Figure 5-7.) Note the classifications assigned to each of these costs. We have predicted their behavior relative to sales revenues or production volume. Our predictions will be used in preparing pro forma statements and cash flow budgets for the firm. As you consider these predictions, remember that cost ratios

FIGURE 5-7 Costs and ratios.

		XYZ Electronics, Inc.	
		Income Statement	
		Last Year	

	Costs in Dollars	Costs in Ratios	Cost classification and predictions
Sales revenues	$211,420	100.0%	—
Material cost	59,410	28.1%	*Variable cost,* gradually increasing, needs to be controlled
Labor cost	69,980	33.1%	*Variable cost,* gradually increasing, needs to be controlled
Shop supervision	12,050	5.7%	*Fixed cost,* can be projected at $1,000/month
Shop overhead	17,130	8.1%	*Semi-fixed cost,* substantially increasing, needs to be controlled
Total mfg. costs	158,570	75.0%	
Gross margin	52,850	25.0%	—
Personal selling	7,820	3.7%	*Discretionary expense,* can be changed to affect sales revenues
Advertising	1,910	0.9%	*Discretionary expense,* can be changed to affect sales revenues
Total selling expenses	9,730	4.6%	
Exec. & staff salaries	22,190	10.5%	*Fixed cost* and a *discretionary expense,* can be changed
Interest expense	7,710	3.7%	*Semi-fixed cost,* can be predicted based on loan size and interest rate
Telephone expense	2,650	1.2%	*Semi-fixed cost,* can be considered to vary with sales revenues
Professional services	3,070	1.4%	*Fixed cost* and a *discretionary expense,* can be changed

	Costs in Dollars	Costs in Ratios	Cost classification and predictions
Office overhead	4,860	2.3%	*Semi-fixed cost,* can be considered to vary with sales revenues
Total admin. expense	40,480	19.1%	
Profits before taxes	2,640	1.3%	—

were computed for 3 prior years to show trends. They were then compared to industry averages to indicate problems. Figure 5-7 omits those trends and comparisons, but they were an essential part of the analysis.

Ratio analysis is used to forecast entries on a pro forma balance sheet. Cost analysis is used to predict the amounts on a pro forma income statement. Preparation of these pro forma financial statements is described in the next section.

EXPECTED FINANCIAL NEEDS

The expected financial needs of a company are based partially on its current financial condition, as determined by ratio analysis and cost analysis, and partially on its proposed marketing plan and production plan. Expected financial needs are analyzed through pro forma financial statements and cash flow budgets.

Pro forma financial statements consist of projected income and cost figures (which estimate the performance of a company over a future time period) and forecasted asset and liability amounts (which indicate the financial condition of the firm at the end of this period). Pro forma statements are used to provide systematic projections of financial needs on a monthly, quarterly, or yearly basis. Consequently, they help anticipate amounts needed from commercial bank loans or venture capital investments.

Assume XYZ Electronics, Inc., has adopted a new strategy that hinges upon an aggressive marketing plan. Company founders expect to substantially increase personal selling and advertising expenses. They believe this expanded marketing effort will result in improved sales revenues and market share. Further assume they have also developed a new frequency synthesizer and market research indicates customers will buy the improved instrument—if made aware of it through sales calls and magazine advertisements.

The first step in preparing pro forma financial statements is to forecast sales revenues. In a beginning firm (with no prior sales to project) or in some existing firms (with a dramatically changing strategy which makes prior sales irrelevant) it is difficult to project these revenues. Be realistic. Support your projections through industry analysis and market research.

We believe XYZ Electronics, Inc., is able to support a projection of sales changing from the current $17,500 per month—gradually over the course of the next year—to $30,000 per month, or $90,000 per quarter. Pro forma statements have been prepared by quarter because of the space limitations on each page.

The second step in preparing pro forma financial statements is to project major variable costs. Assume founders of this company believe they will be able to control material cost to achieve a target of 28.0 percent of sales (versus 27.5 percent for the industry average) and control labor cost to 30.0 percent of sales (versus 29.2 percent for the industry). Smaller variable and semi-fixed costs can be extrapolated as varying directly with sales.

Fixed cost projections are the third and final step. For XYZ Electronics, Inc., these consist of executive and staff salaries, now at $1850 per month. Since these are discretionary expenses, we can assume executives have decided to reduce their salaries, leaving more funds in the firm. By following our several assumptions, all of which seem reasonable to a casual observer, it is possible to prepare the following pro forma income statements and balance sheets (see Figures 5–8 and 5–9).

Pro forma statements show—despite increased profits ($6540 after-tax profits on revenues of $90,000 in the fourth quarter for a return on sales of 7.3 percent) which will be retained in company equity—the firm must be prepared to secure additional financing, probably in the form of an increase in its short-term bank loan. Additional pro forma statements, prepared for the following years, would show when the bank loan could be repaid and when additional investments in productive equipment might have to be made. Pro forma financial statements are essential to the management of high-growth companies.

FIGURE 5-8 Sample pro forma income statement.

XYZ Electronics, Inc.
Pro Forma Income Statement
Next Year

	1st Qtr	2nd Qtr	3rd Qtr	4th Qtr
Sales (gradual increase from present $17,500/month to final $30,000/ month)	57,000	60,000	75,000	90,000
Material cost, at 28.0% of sales	15,960	16,800	21,000	25,200
Labor cost, at 30.0% of sales	17,300	18,000	22,500	27,000
Shop supervision, at $1,000/month	3,000	3,000	3,000	3,000
Shop overhead, at 7.5% of sales	4,270	4,500	5,600	6,700
Total manufacturing costs	40,530	42,300	52,100	61,900
Gross margin	16,470	17,700	22,900	28,100
Personal selling, increase in step-function from present $650/month	3,000	3,000	4,500	4,500
Advertising, incr. in step-function from present $230/month	1,500	3,000	4,500	4,500
Total marketing costs	4,500	6,000	9,000	9,000
Executive salaries, held at $1,500/ month	4,500	4,500	4,500	4,500
Interest expense, on beginning balance:				
bank loan at 9%	560	570	430	660
equipment loan at 12%	610	520	450	370
mortgage loan at 8%	670	650	630	610
Telephone expense, at 1.5% of sales	600	900	1,150	1,350
Professional services, at 1.5%	600	900	1,150	1,350
Office overhead, at 2.0% of sales	1,200	1,200	1,500	1,800
Total administrative expenses	8,740	9,240	9,810	10,640
Profits before taxes	3,230	2,460	4,090	8,460
Federal income taxes, at 25%	810	610	1,020	2,120
Profits after taxes	2,420	1,850	3,070	6,540

Cash flow budgets also are important. They forecast on a weekly or monthly basis cash receipts and payments (rather than accrued revenues and expenses), anticipating momentary cash shortages which might require additional borrowing above that indicated on pro forma financial statements.

FIGURE 5-9 Sample pro forma balance sheet.

XYZ Electronics, Inc.
Pro Forma Balance Sheet
Next Year

Assets	1st Qtr	2nd Qtr	3rd Qtr	4th Qtr
Cash, at minimum balance	3,000	3,000	3,000	3,000
Accts. receivable, at 45 days in 1st qtr., and 40 subsequently	28,500	26,000	32,500	39,000
Inventory, at 70 days in 1st qtr., and 60 subsequently	31,100	27,900	34,400	40,800
Prepaid expenses	2,000	2,000	2,000	2,000
Total current assets	64,600	58,900	71,900	84,800
Equipment, with no new investment	33,200	33,200	33,200	33,200
Depreciation, on 8-year schedule	7,950	9,000	10,050	11,100
Total equipment	25,250	24,200	23,150	22,100
Building, with no new investment	52,000	52,000	52,000	52,000
Depreciation, on 15-year schedule	10,460	11,320	12,180	13,040
Total property	41,540	40,680	39,820	38,960
Total current and fixed assets	131,390	123,780	134,870	145,860
Liabilities				
Accrued salaries and wages	2,000	2,000	2,000	2,000
Accounts payable, at 30 days	7,100	7,500	9,400	11,230
Bank loan—90 day note	25,480	19,180	28,850	35,020
Eqpt loan—current portion; repaid at $2,500 each quarter	10,000	10,000	10,000	10,000
Total current liabilities	44,580	38,680	50,250	58,250
Eqpt loan—2 year contract, transferred to current position	7,500	5,000	2,500	—
Bldg mortgage—paid on an 8 year schedule	32,450	31,400	30,350	29,300
Total long-term debt	39,950	36,400	32,850	29,300
Common stock, with no change	22,000	22,000	22,000	22,000
Retained earnings, with profits	24,860	26,700	29,770	36,310
Total owners equity	46,860	48,700	51,770	58,310
Total liabilities and equity	131,390	123,780	134,870	145,860

A sale is entered in accounting records on the day goods are shipped, not on the day payment is received. A cost is entered on the day shipment occurs, not on the day company workers or suppliers are paid. Cash flow will differ from revenue and expense records.

Cash flow budgets "fill in the blanks" between pro forma balance sheets and income statements. They are prepared over shorter time periods. They reflect actual cash receipts and payments rather than accounting revenues and expenses.

For example, assume founders of XYZ Electronics, Inc., have approached their bank with a request to increase the present $25,000 short-term loan to $35,000 by the end of the year, as shown on the pro forma statements. The loan officer at the bank shows interest in the new product design (improved frequency synthesizer), approves of the more aggressive marketing plan, and is impressed by the detailed pro forma statements provided. But this banker is concerned about possible cash shortages during the first quarter of the plan.

"I don't think you can get through the first 3 months," says the loan officer. "I know you expect to decrease the amounts invested in accounts receivable and in inventory, but you've got to get your accounts payable in better shape or your suppliers will stop shipping to you. And you've got to build up inventory for the increased sales. Your cash flow does not look good."

What do you do when your banker questions cash flow? Prepare a cash flow budget, of course. (You really should have developed one earlier and submitted it with pro forma financial statements as part of the loan request.) It is not difficult. You list your assumptions about expected levels and time intervals of cash receipts and payments, often in comparison to those levels and times for the prior year. Then you compute the expected receipts and payments. (See Figure 5-10.)

The cash flow budget shows a total of $10,000 in short-term financing will be required to get through the first 3 months of the new plan. This cash shortage did not appear on the pro forma financial statements because they were computed by quarter, not by month, and because they reflected accounting revenues and expenses rather than actual cash payments and receipts.

FIGURE 5-10 Sample cash flow budget.

	This Year Average	Jan.	Next Year Feb.	Mar.
XYZ Electronics, Inc.				
Cash Flow Budget				
Assumed sales per month:				
1. Expected sales at current level, adjusted for seasonality	$17,500	$17,500	$17,500	$17,500
2. Increased sales due to the expanded marketing effort		500	1,500	2,500
3. Total sales per month	17,500	18,000	19,000	20,000
Assumed utilization ratios:				
1. Accounts receivable, in days, improved gradually	62.0	55.0	50.0	45.0
2. Inventory, in days, improved gradually	87.0	80.0	75.0	70.0
3. Accounts payable, in days, improved immediately	81.0	30.0	30.0	30.0
Assumed shop material purchases:				
1. Material cost percentage, steady at the current rate	28.1%	28.0%	28.0%	28.0%
2. Material cost dollars, as percentage of expected sales	4,900	5,000	5,300	5,600
3. Decreased purchases due to use of inventory (20 work days/mo.)				
7 day improvement in January		−1,800		
5 day improvement in February			−1,300	
5 day improvement in March				−1,400
4. Consequent purchases of shop materials	4,900	3,200	3,700	3,600
Assumed shop employment costs:				
1. Labor cost percentage, improved from the current rate	33.1%	32.0%	30.0%	30.0%
2. Labor cost dollars, as percentage of expected sales per month	6,000	5,800	5,500	6,000
Cash receipts from accounts receivable:				
1. Normal collection of prior 30 days sales	17,500	17,500	18,000	19,000

	This Year Average	Jan.	Next Year Feb.	Mar.
2. Increased collections due to new control procedures				
7 day improvement in January		+4,100		
5 day improvement in February			+2,900	
5 day improvement in March				+2,900
3. Total cash receipts expected per month	17,500	21,600	20,900	21,900
Cash disbursements for accounts payable:				
1. Normal payments for prior 30 days shop material purchases	4,900	4,900	3,200	3,700
2. Normal payments for prior 30 days shop overhead purchases	1,400	1,400	1,400	1,400
3. Normal payments for prior 30 days office overhead purchases	400	400	400	400
4. Increased payments to bring to 30 days status to preserve credit		14,100		
5. Total cash disbursements expected per month	6,700	20,800	5,000	5,500
Cash disbursements for general expenses:				
1. Shop supervision salaries	1,000	1,000	1,000	1,000
2. Personal selling and travel	650	1,000	1,000	1,000
3. Advertising and promotion	230	500	500	500
4. Executive and staff salaries	1,850	1,500	1,500	1,500
5. Interest charges	650	700	700	700
6. Telephone expenses	220	200	200	200
7. Professional services	250	200	200	200
8. Total cash disbursement expected per month	4,850	5,100	5,100	5,100
Total cash receipts and disbursements:				
1. Cash receipts from accounts receivable	17,500	21,600	20,900	21,900
2. Cash disbursements for shop labor payroll	6,000	5,800	5,500	6,000
3. Cash disbursements for accounts payable	6,700	20,800	5,000	5,500
4. Cash disbursements for general expenses	4,850	5,100	5,100	5,100
5. Balance of receipts and disbursements and cash surplus (shortage)	(50)	(10,000)	5,300	5,300

POSSIBLE FINANCIAL SOURCES

A high-growth firm's needs for funds, as we previously explained, are dependent upon marketing and production plans as projected by pro forma financial statements and cash flow budgets. Possible sources of needed funds include personal and family advances, commercial bank loans, and venture capital investments.

Personal and family advances are the most common source of financing for small businesses. New company founders typically invest a substantial portion of their own savings in the venture to get it started and often leave all of the profits and much of their salaries in the firm to keep it going. They also may ask friends and relatives to advance funds for company use.

We *strongly suggest* that amounts borrowed from relatives and friends be kept to an absolute minimum. Reduce the level of funding required, if necessary, by readjusting your marketing and production plans. Why? Because your new company will become successful or unsuccessful, depending in large measure upon the quality of your planning.

If your venture is unsuccessful, friends and relatives will lose their investments. Many older people, particularly parents and in-laws, may be badly hurt by such a loss. Close friends and relatives never seem to think about the possibility of loss until it occurs, and then they may find their own plans for retirement must be drastically altered. It would be very awkward and unpleasant to tell an elderly relative you have lost a substantial portion of their life savings. Do not borrow money from older people unless they can easily sustain the loss.

If, on the other hand, your company is successful, friends and relatives who made advances will be delighted—for a while. Relatives may agree to accept repayment of their loan funds with interest, but friends are likely to feel that because they shared the risks, they should now share the rewards. A new venture start-up or a high-growth firm expansion requires both emotional and financial commitments. Many friendships do not survive those commitments. Use your own money and professional sources of funds. Two professional sources of funds are commercial banks and venture capitalists.

COMMERCIAL BANK LOANS

Many founders of new ventures are discouraged by their initial reception at a commercial bank. They arrange a meeting with bank officers at which they describe their products, explain their markets, outline their plans, and request a loan. The loan request seems to disappear into a financial maze.

Occasionally, further information is requested by bank officers or additional security is demanded. The bank's response often is delayed until company plans must be changed or other sources considered. By the time a sought-after loan is granted, founders often feel they have been badly treated. And, of course, many loans requested by new businesses are simply not granted.

There are several reasons for this hesitant reception. Start-up ventures generally lack an operating history for prospective lenders to study; this makes it difficult to appraise company management and the competitive position of the firm. Also, new companies frequently have only indefinite or imprecise assets to offer as security for a loan. Finally (and most telling), fledgling companies tend to go bankrupt more often than large, established firms.

Commercial banks do grant loans to new ventures, but usually they insist upon a well-prepared loan request which will stand up under rigorous examination. Most new entrepreneurs do not know how to prepare such a loan request, and most bankers neglect to explain the loan review process. The result is an almost classic communication breakdown. Budding entrepreneurs, by and large, believe commercial bankers evaluating loans still rely on the traditional "three Cs" of character, capital, and collateral. Yet, today's bankers generally admit: Character is difficult to judge in beginning companies; capital is often limited in high-growth situations; and collateral may be of questionable value under conditions of rapid technological and economic change. Bankers now prefer to look at the following factors in deciding whether or not to approve a loan: past operations, loan purpose, repayment schedule, and company future. The loan request, therefore, has to address each of these topics.

1. **Past operations.** Most banks want audited financial statements covering at least 3 years of operations. In the review process, credit

analysts will examine the growth of sales and profits and the liquidity and debt positions of the firm. But they will be more interested in knowing how well company management has used available resources. These credit analysts will carefully scrutinize the aging of accounts receivable, the turnover of inventory, the return on assets, and so on. Since analysts can be expected to note changes in ratios over the history of the company and compare ratios to published industry averages, a well-prepared loan request should include calculated ratios, industry comparisons, and explanations of any obvious trends or meaningful differences between company and industry figures.

We suggest you provide audited financial statements for 3 years of operations. These statements do not necessarily have to be formally audited, with an opinion on their accuracy expressed by a certified public accountant. They should be prepared (or at least reviewed) by an accountant external to the firm and, it is hoped, one who is known and respected by officers of the bank.

For genuine start-up firms, it obviously is impossible to provide a 3-year history of operations. Most banks do not like to deal with beginning companies because of this lack of data upon which to form a judgment. In such instances, bank officers will generally weigh the prior experience and personal financial worth of founders and ask for personal guarantees of the business loan. A well-prepared loan request in such cases should contain resumes of founders, detailed records of their personal property, and indications of their willingness to provide personal guarantees.

Personal guarantees may become a sticking point for the new entrepreneur and his or her associates. They often become a sticking point for bankers, too. A typical response by a loan officer to your refusal to provide a guarantee is: "If you don't have faith in your proposal, you can't expect us to have faith in it, and we won't grant the loan."

2. **Loan purpose.** Most banks want specific information on the full amount of the loan requested and the expected use of the funds—expressed as proportions to be devoted to capital investments and current assets. Loan officers are particularly interested in gauging whether the amount requested will be adequate for the purpose envisaged; otherwise supplemental loan appeals may have to be considered later. When a banker asks you and other new company

founders if you are certain the amount requested is large enough, it should not be construed as a generous offer of additional funds. More often it is a plea for reassurance that company management has considered all possible increases in costs and all probable delays in receipt of revenues associated with the loan project. A detailed cash flow budget will provide this reassurance and specifically indicate the use of the funds. A well-prepared loan request also should contain a narrative description of the project—market expansion or production improvement—and explain foreseeable problems.

In dealings with commercial banks, the loan purpose must be either sales expansion or process improvement. Banks may advance funds for physical facilities (needed for marketing or production) and for working capital (used to support changes in marketing or production) because these generate tangible assets (plant and equipment, process inventory, and accounts receivable) which can be pledged as security for the loan. Banks will not consider advancing funds for product development or advertising programs which generate intangible assets (capitalized research and development expenses or goodwill). Commercial bankers expect product and market development activities of beginning companies to be financed by the equity funds of owners and investors.

3. **Repayment schedule.** Most banks want definite information on the time period over which the loan will be outstanding and the proposed repayment method. Bank officers are particularly interested in making certain repayment can be made from the normal cash flow of the loan project, without impairing normal company operations. Even though most loans do generate tangible assets, bankers do not want to rely upon liquidation of those assets for repayment because it would defeat the purpose of the loan.

A well-prepared loan request should contain monthly or quarterly pro forma financial statements, extending over the life of the loan, showing expected revenues generated by the loan project and the effect of repayment on the operations and financial condition of the firm. A narrative discussion of the repayment schedule also should be included, offering some consideration of "best case" and "worst case" scenarios.

In the best case, sales might expand so rapidly that scheduled repayment funds would have to be retained by the company to finance accounts receivable. In the worst case, sales might decline so far that loan project funds generated would be inadequate for repayment. Experienced bank officers recognize that economic conditions change, and they believe their customers should anticipate probable consequences of those changes.

At most commercial banks, the length of the loan cannot exceed 3 years. Bank officers typically believe funds for equipment purchases or working capital increases should provide an adequate cash flow for reasonably prompt repayment. General purpose machines with immediate resale value provide one exception to this rule of thumb; they might be financed for 5 years. Buildings and real estate constitute a second exception and might be mortgaged for 12 to 15 years. (In most cases, one commercial bank will seek participation by other lenders when making real estate loans.) Seasonal inventory or accounts receivable financing offer a third exception, although on the other end of the scale; seasonal loans usually are expected to be repaid within 12 months.

4. **Company future.** Most banks do not advance funds to small and beginning companies because the current loan is profitable; bank profit on these loans often is minimal (despite a higher-than-prime interest rate) because of the small amounts involved and increased expenses for investigation and administration. Instead, most bankers make loans to start-up ventures because they expect to witness company growth and eventual bank profits from expanded customer deposits and on-going relationships.

A well-prepared loan request should include a brief description of company objectives. It also should include a statement of the general direction founders plan to follow—after loan repayment— in product development, market expansion, or process improvements. Bank officers like to believe their loans generate increased economic activity in the community and personal financial success for company owners.

Commercial banks represent just one of many types of financial institutions in the nation, but they also constitute the major source of loan funds for small or beginning businesses. Most other financial institutions, such as insurance companies or brokerage firms, simply refuse to deal with smaller companies because of the greater risks entailed and increased time required for loan processing. Still others, such as finance companies, state and local development agencies, and the U.S. Small Business Administration, do make loans to smaller companies, but often in participation with a local commercial bank. The local bank is expected to act as administrator and contact point for these loans.

New company founders should make a special effort to establish a good working relationship with one commercial bank. This is not difficult. You do not need a charismatic personality nor a large entertainment budget. Just provide your banker with explicit and detailed financial projections in loan requests. Then submit accurate and timely financial statements each month, showing progress in meeting your projections. Few beginning companies are willing to take the time to keep bank officers so fully informed. Bank officers tend to value those who do.

VENTURE CAPITAL INVESTMENTS

Venture capitalists are the second major source of capital for high-growth companies, following commercial banks. The entrepreneur should understand the typical decision processes of venture capital firms and individual investors. Both are potential sources of equity investments. Most importantly, you should know how to apply for and negotiate terms of those funds.

As with commercial banks, many high-growth company founders are disappointed by the results of initial contacts with venture capitalists. Entrepreneurs often feel their proposals are brusquely rejected without careful consideration. Alternatively, they may believe venture capitalists demand too much equity or expect too great a return on their prospective investment. A frequently mentioned capital gain target is 500 percent in 5 years.

Venture capital firms and individual investors do not realize large returns on all investments, and those investments which actually do return capital gains of 500 percent in 5 years are notable exceptions. Yet, they search for venture projects with such a substantial appreciation potential to make up for the considerable share of their investments which prove unsuccessful. Venture capital is a risky business.

Casual observers tend to hear about the industry's successes—the Apple Computers and Tandem Computers—but not the failures. Failures frequently do occur. After all, judging the potential of small or beginning companies is not easy. Most venture capital firms follow a set of established policies concerning venture proposal size, timing, management, and distinctive quality; this helps improve their judgments and reduce their risks. High-growth company founders who want to apply for equity financing from a venture capitalist should understand and conform to these policies.

SIZE OF THE VENTURE PROPOSAL

Most venture capital firms show interest in investment projects with a value of $250,000 to $1,500,000. Smaller projects are of limited interest because of high costs of investigation and administration.

A typical venture capital firm receives more than 1000 proposals every year. Some 30 percent of them are quickly rejected because they do not fit established industrial or technological fields of interest. (Many firms invest only in certain industries, such as health care or telecommunications.) Another 60 percent or more are promptly turned away because they are the wrong size or have been poorly prepared. The remaining 10 percent or so are investigated with care. This investigation tends to be expensive.

Venture capital is a labor-intensive business. Proposed product characteristics often must be evaluated by a panel of consultants, particularly if the product has high technological or innovative content. Market size normally is estimated by a market research firm through industry analysis and customer contacts. Next, the production method is reviewed by industrial engineers, who confirm production costs. Finally, the character and competence of founding management is investigated by one partner of the venture capital firm.

Preliminary investigation costs about $10,000 to $15,000 per project; it results in the screening out of all but perhaps 10 to 15 proposals in which the firm takes a definite interest. A second investigation, more thorough and expensive than the first, reduces the number under consideration to three or four. Eventually, the venture capital firm invests in one or two of these. Partners in most venture capital firms feel they cannot afford to consider proposals of under $250,000.

TIMING OF THE VENTURE PROPOSAL

Most venture capital firms show interest in negotiating investment projects with successful, operating companies. The ideal situation may involve an established firm which enjoys market demand considerably exceeding supply; venture capitalists can provide funds for expanded capacity and increased working capital, resulting in rapid growth. A second-most-attractive proposition may come from a profitable company wishing to develop a related product line or expand into an adjacent market segment; venture capitalists can provide needed funds, enabling the firm to grow in step function or faster than on the normal compound curve of retained earnings.

Companies with developed products but lacking funds for manufacturing and marketing those products probably constitute a third tier of attractiveness. Next on the list are companies—or more often groups of people planning to start a company—which have an idea for a product and insufficient development funds; venture capitalists can provide money for research and development but generally do so only to people with established product design reputations and only for products with unquestionable growth potential. Last on the investment attractiveness list are companies with severe financial problems; venture capitalists rarely provide funds to correct other peoples' mistakes.

There is a natural sequence which can help predict the willingness of venture capital firms to provide funds. It is based upon ease of investigation and certainty of success. Companies enjoying growing market demand but suffering from inadequate productive capacity are easier to evaluate and more certain of success than groups of people with a product idea. The following series of questions—which an entrepreneur can ask himself or herself—may help you to determine the likely response of venture capital firms to your investment proposal.

1. **Product.** Do you have a prototype? Does it work?
2. **Market.** Have you made some sales? Are your customers enthusiastic?
3. **Process.** Are you manufacturing regularly? Can your existing process be expanded or must it be totally redesigned for volume production?
4. **Money.** Do you have adequate financing for the next few months? Does it appear demand is rapidly growing, so you will need additional financing soon after this period?
5. **Reputation.** Are you well known within your industry? Have you previously participated in a start-up venture?

A person who can truthfully answer "yes" to all questions may be able to pick and choose among venture capital sources. Someone who can answer "yes" to the first three groups of questions probably will be able to raise venture capital on terms he or she will consider reasonable. A person who can answer "yes" to just the first one or two questions may search far and wide for venture capital and still not find it.

REQUIREMENTS OF THE VENTURE PROPOSAL

Most venture capital firms show interest in the competence and character of management. They believe even mediocre products can be successfully manufactured, promoted, and distributed by an energetic and experienced management team. They look for such teams, with demonstrated ability to work together smoothly and productively even under conditions of stress. Venture capital financing is offered only to companies with perceived managerial competence. Verbal offers may hinge upon successful new management talent recruitment. But contracts seldom are signed until the new talent is on board.

Evaluation of managerial competence is usually the last step in considering a venture capital investment. A partner or senior executive of the venture capital firm often will spend several days at the offices of a company being considered for equity financing, talking with and observing its management. This potential investor normally expects that the target company possesses a complete management group with training, experience, and assigned responsibilities in all of the major functional areas of product design, marketing, production, finance, and control. He or she will insist that each member of the management group must have a thorough understanding of the industry and evidence a high degree of commitment to the company.

EVALUATION OF THE VENTURE PROPOSAL

Most venture capital firms also look for two distinctive elements of company strategy. First is a reason for success at the start that is based upon a gap in the product line, a niche in the market segmentation, or an opportunity in the production process. Second is a competitive advantage over the long run—some product, market, or process edge which will prevent other firms from simply copying the new product, market, or process concept. Here, of course, we refer to the importance of industry analysis and strategic positioning of a start-up firm within your chosen industry.

EQUITY FINANCING PROPOSAL

Once investigation of a particular venture has been completed and a decision to invest in the equity of this company has been made, venture capital firms typically prepare an equity financing proposal. It details the amount of money to be provided, the percentage of common stock to be surrendered in exchange for these funds, the interim financing method to be used, and the protective covenants (rules of conduct) to be included. This proposal will be discussed with the management of the company, and the final financing arrangement will be a compromise between owners of the company and partners of the venture capital firm. Important dimensions of the compromise are ownership, control, annual charges, and final objectives.

1. **Ownership.** Venture capital financing is not inexpensive for small business owners; venture capital firm partners insist upon a percentage of equity in exchange for their investment funds. This percentage of equity varies, depending upon the amount of money provided and the current size and prior success record of the business. It can vary from perhaps 10 percent in the case of an established, successful company up to 75 percent or more for beginning or financially troubled firms. Most venture capital firms determine the ratio of the funds provided to equity requested by comparison of the present financial worth of the contributions by each of the parties to the agreement. The present financial worth of contributions by founders of a beginning company is often valued at a minimal amount; usually it is estimated at just the existing value of their idea and the competitive costs of their time. The present financial worth of contributions by owners of an established, successful firm is valued much higher; it is often capitalized at a multiple of current stock earnings. Applicants for venture capital should be aware of a third method of valuing a firm, called "discounting" the projected earnings. See Appendix B for a detailed explanation of this method.

Financial valuation is not an exact science. The final compromise on value in the equity financing agreement is likely to be much lower than company founders think it should be and considerably higher than venture capital firm partners believe it might be. Yet ideally, the two parties to the compromise will be able to do together what neither could do alone. The company should be able to grow fast enough with the additional funds to more than overcome the owners' loss of equity. The investment should be able to grow at the same rate, repaying the venture capitalists' assumption of risk. An equity financing agreement which pleases both parties by its outcome in 3 to 5 years is perfect. But such an agreement is often difficult to arrange.

Company founders seeking equity financing should consider the ratio of funds invested to ownership requested not only under current circumstances but also as it may be affected by future conditions and growth.

2. **Control.** Issues of control are more easily resolved than those of ownership. Unlike the division of equity—upon which both parties are bound to disagree—venture capitalists and company founders share a common, though perhaps unapparent, interest in control. Despite the natural fears and worries of high-growth company founders, venture capital firm partners have little interest in assuming control of the business. They have neither the technical expertise nor the managerial personnel to run a number of small companies in diverse industries. Venture capitalists prefer to leave operating control to the existing management. Venture capitalists usually do want to participate in any strategic decisions which might change the basic product-market character of the company, however, and in any major investment choices which might divert or deplete the financial resources of the company.

Venture capital investors generally ask that at least one partner of their firm be made a director of the company. Venture capital partners also want the contractual right to assume control and attempt to rescue their investment if severe financial, operating, or marketing problems develop. They usually include protective covenants in the equity financing agreement which permit them to take control (and appoint new officers) under circumstances such as a drop in working capital below a given amount or a lag in sales below a stated annual forecast.

Company founders seeking equity financing should consider the exact wording and general intent of protective covenants contained in the financing agreement.

3. **Annual charges.** Venture capital investments may be made in the form of direct stock ownership, which does not impose annual fixed charges. But a more common method of investment is in the form of "convertible subordinated debentures"; these debentures may be exchanged, at an established rate, for common stock. The convertible feature of the investment instrument permits the venture capital partners to realize their capital gains (at their option) in the future. Subordinated means that all existing and planned debt takes precedence in the event of liquidation, allowing the company to obtain additional bank financing. The debenture form of investment provides further security and control for venture capital partners, but it also imposes a fixed charge for interest (and sometimes principal) upon the company.

Company founders seeking equity financing should consider the current and future burden represented by any fixed annual charges contained in the financing agreement.

4. **Final objectives.** The goal of the venture capital firm, generally, is to realize a capital gain from its investment by either arranging a public offering of company stock or by merging the company with a larger firm which has publicly traded stock at some time in the future, usually within 3 to 5 years. Most equity financing agreements will include provisions guaranteeing participation by the venture capital firm in any stock sale or merger decisions. The agreement may explicitly state: Company management must work toward an eventual stock sale or merger.

Company founders seeking equity financing should consider the eventual impact of a public stock sale or merger upon their own stock holdings and personal ambitions, e.g., few founding company officers continue to hold their jobs for long following a merger.

There are a number of different types of venture capital firms. They tend to be concentrated in locations where many established high-growth companies exist and where start-up firms are proliferating. There are numerous publications that list the names and addresses of venture capital firms, but these tend to become obsolete fairly quickly as new companies enter the market and old partnerships become

more conservative and drop out. Most commercial bankers can provide
you with the names of local venture capital firms, or you can write to
the national associations and ask for a list of their members. There are
three associations:

1. National Association of Small Business Investment Companies
   618 Washington Building
   Washington, D.C. 20005
2. National Venture Capital Association
   1225 19th Street, NW, Suite 750
   Washington, D.C. 20036
3. Western Association of Venture Capitalists
   300 Sand Hill Road
   Menlo Park, CA 94025

New venture capital firms are emerging throughout the nation, often
in areas where economic growth is needed.

1. **Traditional venture partnerships** sprang up in the 1960s or earlier and are backed by wealthy families, aggressively managing a
   portion of their inherited funds. They invest primarily in established
   high-growth firms.
2. **Professional venture partnerships** were created by financial
   managers with prior experience in banks or traditional venture
   capital firms. These partnerships do not invest their own capital;
   they raise it from wealthy individuals, insurance firms, and other
   sources.
3. **Investment banking firms** normally trade in more established
   securities, but occasionally put together a syndicate of investors for
   venture capital proposals. Often their investments are considered to
   be of a high-risk, high-return nature. These firms sometimes invest
   in start-up businesses.
4. **Large manufacturing companies** periodically make investments
   in smaller firms as a means of supplementing their own internal
   research and development capabilities. These companies, more often than other types of venture capitalists, are likely to invest on the
   strength of product development and venture start-up proposals.
5. **Commercial banks** have started approximately 300 venture capital
   firms nationally to supplement their normal loan and lease financing businesses. These firms are wholly owned by the bank but are

often legally registered as small business investment companies (S.B.I.C.s), which permits borrowing from the federal government at low interest rates.

In addition to the various types of venture capital firms, there are a large number of private individuals interested in the potential gains represented by high-growth companies. Many of these persons have adequate financial resources to provide equity financing. Amounts may be limited, however, particularly for second- and third-round financing of very successful or very troubled ventures. Finally there are "finders"—often law partnerships or financial advisors—who do not have the personal resources for direct investment but are acquainted with people who do. They frequently offer to help (with varying degrees of effectiveness and honesty) founders of high-growth companies seeking equity financing.

Partners and managers of venture capital firms receive many more proposals than they can consider each year, and they consider many more than they can finance. All have been exposed to the enthusiasm and optimistic forecasts of new company founders, and they tend to quickly reject venture proposals which fail to meet minimum requirements: adequate size, successful operation, experienced and competent management, and a distinctive product.

All in all, it is difficult for many entrepreneurs to obtain financing needed for growth, either in the form of short-term loans from commercial banks or long-term equity from venture capital firms. Well-prepared proposals can help you to overcome the initial scepticism of financing professionals. The core of such a proposal is your financial plan. It analyzes your company's current financial position, projects future financial needs, and explores sources of financing which match specific needs. The various steps in financial planning, presented in Figure 5-1, should be referred to again for emphasis.

CHAPTER SIX
ORGANIZATIONAL PLANNING

Organizational planning is often neglected by new company founders. Formation team members spend their time on marketing plans, production plans, and financial plans because they are needed immediately; the company cannot start until these plans are completed. What founders frequently forget is that nothing will happen in marketing, production, and finance unless someone makes it happen.

At the last minute formation team members, friends, and acquaintances may be assigned to management posts—without receiving any direction on what is to be done, in what sequence, by what time, and at what cost. The result is a lack of coordination between managers and a lack of progress by the company. Organizational plans for start-up ventures are important.

For new businesses, organizational plans are dependent upon pre-existing plans for marketing, production, and finance. Each of these earlier plans create a number of tasks to be accomplished. These tasks—adjusted for relationships between them and people available to perform them—determine the design of an organizational structure and the development of management systems for planning, control, and motivation. This view of the organizational planning process is shown graphically in Figure 6-1.

Tasks to be accomplished include decisions and actions which must be done thoughtfully and attentively for the company to succeed. The organizational structure assigns responsibility for each of these tasks to specific management positions. It then delineates lines of communication and patterns of authority between positions.

A company's "planning system" sets reasonably flexible goals for the performance of tasks and responds to changes in the marketplace or in the business environment. A firm's "control system" compares

FIGURE 6-1 Process of organizational design.

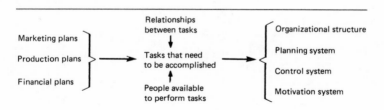

planned goals to actual outcomes so that corrective action can be promptly taken. An organization's "motivational system" creates and dispenses incentives and rewards for achieving planned goals. All are needed—a clearly defined organizational structure and formal systems of planning, control, and motivation—for coordinated, effective start-up venture management. Once a company becomes successful and patterns of communication and decision-making become habitual, then the structure can be relaxed and the systems deformalized. At the start, they have to be there.

TASKS TO BE ACCOMPLISHED

There are some functional tasks which must be well done for a company to succeed, and there are a great many others which can be done in a relatively routine fashion. The first step in organizational planning is to define the ones which have to be well done. Review your marketing, production, and financial plans. For each, ask yourself: "What has to be accomplished to make this plan work? What are the critical decisions and actions needed to transform this proposal from a sterile set of ideas on paper into an on-going, successful, functional department inside your new company?" Imagine an initial customer contact. Think through the sequence of activities required for a single sale: processing the order, shipping the goods, recording the invoice, analyzing the costs. What will make that customer tell his or her neighbors and associates that your company is outstanding?

Concentrate on critical tasks, not the routine ones. Every company has to have a payroll, for example, but this normally is not particularly important. Much more critical in the finance departments of most firms is credit approval, records maintenance, costs analysis, and cash-flow forecasts. (For some small companies in labor-intensive service industries, payroll supervision might become a critical task. Use your own judgment.)

Define "do-able tasks," jobs that can be done by people assigned to them. Think about what you may be asking when you tell a person he or she is in charge of a specific activity or responsible for a given decision. Can that person directly accomplish what you ask? Or is what you are asking for a result of other people's activities? Establishing price levels is do-able, for example. Setting up distributors is do-able. Starting an advertising program is, too. Yet, increasing sales revenues is not do-able; it occurs as the result of other decisions and actions.

You *can* assign a person responsibility for integrating the marketing program, which includes pricing, distribution, and promotion. You *can* measure the performance of that person against increases or decreases in sales revenues. But you should not assign the *task* of increasing sales revenues because it is not a decision or action by itself. (The reason we draw this distinction will become clear through discussion of organizational-structure design and planning- and control-systems development.)

To illustrate the process of defining critical, do-able tasks, let us turn back to the same hypothetical example used throughout the preceding chapter on financial planning. XYZ Electronics, Inc., is a small company, already in business but doing poorly. The firm manufactures electronic test equipment, particularly frequency counters and frequency synthesizers. Company founders expanded their manufacturing capacity too rapidly and were forced to cut personal selling and advertising expenditures to save funds. They also had lost sales momentum and now were losing money. In an attempt to rescue the firm, XYZ Electronics' managers had developed a much-improved model of one of their test instruments. They planned to market this product aggressively, produce it efficiently, and turn their losses into profits.

What are the critical tasks for XYZ Electronics? It is possible to list them under each of the three major functional areas, as shown in Figure 6-2. If the new product is as good as the founders believe, if the market is as large as they think, and if everyone enthusiastically performs the tasks they have been assigned, the company probably will succeed.

FIGURE 6-2 Critical tasks by functional area.

Marketing tasks	Production tasks	Financial tasks
Contact customers	Schedule operations	Maintain records
Engage distributors	Train workers	Analyze costs
Prepare advertising	Control costs	Project cash flows
Process orders	Ship promptly	Arrange bank loans

PEOPLE AVAILABLE TO PERFORM TASKS

People differ in their functional and technical abilities, intelligence levels, creative capacities, and other personal characteristics. You do not need to read a book on high-growth ventures to discover this basic fact. Yet, a new venture is at a disadvantage in working with these differences among people. You may not have considered this fact before.

In an established firm, the abilities and characteristics of employees become known and accepted. People are promoted into jobs for which (if the company is well managed) they have demonstrated competence. Sales representatives often are promoted to sales manager, for example, after they have shown they are good at selling a product. Product designers are promoted to chief engineer after they have demonstrated they are adept at designing a product. There are well-known problems with this approach, of course. Ability at selling does not immediately translate into ability at managing sales people or in developing sales programs, but it is a reasonable indication. Beginning business firms do not receive such indications.

Company founders cannot observe employees at work, designing, producing, and selling *their* products. People have to be recruited from outside the company and placed in positions of responsibility without providing direct evidence of their abilities. They now may be working at closely similar tasks at other companies in the same industry or they may be working at roughly similar jobs in a different industry or they may just be working in similar functional departments such as marketing or finance. Many people want to go to work for smaller companies to escape the bureaucracy and regimentation of large corporations, and many more would like to be hired by start-up ventures to "get in on the ground floor." All of these prospective employees tend to believe their expertise is transferable.

A problem often faced by beginning firms is that general experience is not always quickly transferable. An extended learning period may be needed, and new ventures do not have the time to train employees. Engineers and managers must be able to contribute from the start. We strongly recommend, therefore, that you search for candidates with exceptional job experience and observable competence. They should offer convincing evidence that they did well in past assignments in the same or a closely similar industry. We also recommend that you find and consider at least three interested candidates for each position. Select the one who seems best qualified.

Do not stop searching when you have located an apparently qualified individual; you need at least two others to provide standards upon which to gauge qualifications. Do not hire next-door neighbors or relatives who promise to work hard unless they meet or exceed those standards. Initial staffing is one of the most critical decision phases in the formation of your new company. Give it the time and care it deserves.

RELATIONSHIP BETWEEN TASKS

Critical tasks within an organization—those jobs or activities which must be well done for marketing, production, and financial plans to work together—are interrelated. These interrelationships stem from the flow of material through the production process and the flow of information through the management process. Both flows, of material and information, must be reflected in the design of the organizational structure. Both affect the way in which people within an organization behave toward one another. A person whose job performance is dependent upon receiving either material or information from another person, for example, will tend to communicate often with that person. The organizational structure should facilitate, rather than obstruct, such communication.

Material flow through the production process of a small company tends to be relatively direct. There may be just one product line and one production process. The flow of material can be easily traced. In large, established firms, material flow can become incredibly complex, with raw materials and components moving back and forth between divisions. Where do raw materials or purchased components come from? What further processing is done within the company? Where is assembly performed? Testing? Packaging and shipment?

To examine material flow in your own company, first review the operational analysis section of your production plan, which should have identified the sequence of processing and assembly operations necessary to produce your good or service. Then, see if this sequence naturally fits within one of the major functional areas. For XYZ Electronics, Inc., the operational sequence, or material flow, seems to fit naturally within production. (See Figure 6-3.)

Information flow within a small firm is somewhat more complex than the flow of material in the production process. List the major functional areas: marketing, production, and finance. Examine the various types of information transferred back and forth between departments. Who has to tell what to whom to make things go? For XYZ Electronics, Inc., the flow of information is relatively direct and obvious. (See Figure 6-4.)

Our hypothetical company is shipping standardized test and measurement instruments from inventory. Think about how much more complex the transfers of information might become if it was manufacturing nonstandardized test and measurement systems to match customers' order specifications. Each customer inquiry would move to engineering for preliminary design, to finance for bid preparation, to production for delivery estimation, and then back to marketing for communication of all this information to the customer. Because few designs for specialized electronic systems are accepted in the first go-around, it is likely that the design-bid-schedule process would be repeated, with increasing urgency, up to a final deadline. It probably would be necessary to assign a project leader for each customer inquiry—to coordinate and expedite the marketing, production, finance,

---

FIGURE 6-3 Flow of material through the production process.

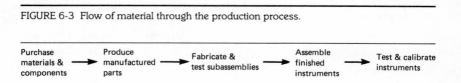

FIGURE 6-4 Flow of information between functional departments.

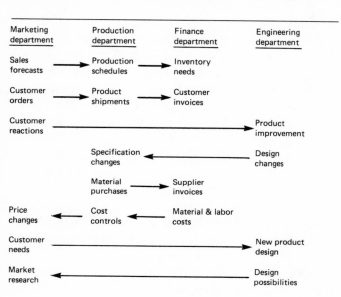

Marketing department	Production department	Finance department	Engineering department
Sales forecasts	Production schedules	Inventory needs	
Customer orders	Product shipments	Customer invoices	
Customer reactions			Product improvement
	Specification changes		Design changes
	Material purchases	Supplier invoices	
Price changes	Cost controls	Material & labor costs	
Customer needs			New product design
Market research			Design possibilities

and engineering activities involved in the preparation of customer proposals.

Recognize the information flows imposed by the competitive strategy of your firm and add those information flows to your organization's structure and management systems. Information flow can become more complex with alterations in competitive strategy. It also can become more complicated with each addition to product line, market segments, geographic territory, or process technology. Such changes occur with growth—following successful company establishment—as new product lines are designed, new market segments served, new district offices opened, or new technologies investigated. You should consider the possibility of such changes at the start, before finalizing your organizational-structure design.

DESIGN OF THE ORGANIZATIONAL STRUCTURE

There are two reasons for development of a formal organizational structure, or hierarchical chart, in a start-up venture. First, it assigns responsibility for critical task performance to specific positions in the structure. Second, it helps ensure that each person within the organization clearly understands his or her responsibilities.

Smaller companies often enjoy tremendous enthusiasm and spirit among functional and technical personnel. Everyone wants the venture to succeed. Everyone is willing to do that extra bit to ensure it does succeed. Unfortunately, the extra bit may involve stepping on someone else's toes. Conflicts arise. Overlaps occur. Some truly important tasks fall aside. Much of this can be avoided by designing a formal organizational structure, with assigned responsibilities, at the start.

Formal organizational-structure design is not easy, nor is there ever a single solution. Numerous assignments of critical tasks are possible and various relationships between the functional and technical positions may be considered. The essential design criterion is to generate a logic—in the assignments and in the relationships—that will be apparent to the people who must make the structure and the company work.

Start by grouping your critical tasks within the major functional and technical areas, paying special attention to any problems caused by different product lines, market segments, geographic locations, production processes, or technological competencies. If more than one of these variables is involved in a single position (unlikely but possible in start-up ventures), you may want to split assignments and set up two positions rather than one.

Next, look at the material flow within the production process. Can all of this be kept within one functional area, probably production? For most companies such an arrangement is possible, but for others— particularly service businesses—the "product" is going to be split by responsibilities for customer contact, operations management, and customer delivery. Some of the necessary activities may fall under marketing and some under production. For example, consider the flow of "material" in providing investment counseling and tax planning services to middle-income clients; it is hard to judge where marketing leaves off and production begins.

Now, look at the information flow between functional and technical areas. Your objective should be to keep information transfer as direct as possible, preferably between positions on the same organizational level. Finally, begin to think about problems of coordinating critical task performance. Coordination often is accomplished by establishing a hierarchical level, or a general management position, above the functional and technical units. The general manager, the president in most small companies, normally assumes responsibility for profit performance and public representation.

Coordination of critical tasks and integration of assigned personnel also can be accomplished by less-authoritarian solutions such as informal meetings, formal committees, project teams, and product managers. Again, the intent of organizational design is to make certain that people know what their responsibilities are and how they should interact with each other in performing them.

The formal structure most likely to result from this process of task-definition and relationship-analysis, for smaller firms and start-up ventures, is called "functional." (See Figure 6-5.) It is the simplest form available. A functional structure consists of a single directive position—the president or general manager—and separate functional and technical departments for such activities as marketing, production, finance, and engineering. Often, coordinating committees are established for product planning (product development and market expansion) and corporate planning (strategic objectives, resource allocations, and revenue-expense budgets).

The advantage of functional structure is its simplicity, with clearly assigned responsibilities and direct communication channels. The disadvantage is that it may be too simplistic. Functional organizations are suitable only for small companies with a single product line or for somewhat larger firms with closely related multiple product lines. Functional structure does not work well for unrelated, multiple prod-

FIGURE 6-5 Typical functional organization.

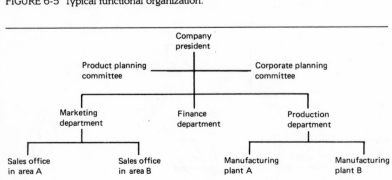

uct lines because people within the organization constantly have to switch their attention back and forth between products. This creates problems of communication and coordination.

A "divisional" structure commonly is used by companies which have two or more dissimilar product lines, aimed at different market segments and manufactured by different production processes. (See Figure 6-6.) Each division in the structure is assigned responsibility for a single product or product line and is allocated adequate resources in production, distribution, and promotion to successfully manufacture and market that product. It is possible to think of each division as a separate functional organization. But, generally, activities common to all divisions, such as finance, personnel, and (if technologies are similar) engineering, are drawn away from the divisions and centralized at the corporate level.

The advantage of the divisional organization is its assignment of profit responsibility for each product line to a single individual, the division manager. The disadvantage is that manufacturing and marketing functions are decentralized, reporting to division managers and not to the corporate president. Consequently, synergism, the sharing of joint resources, becomes very difficult. Isolation of units in a divisional structure seems to defeat efforts towards achieving economies of scale and scope. Joint use of similar production facilities or distribution channels rarely happens.

The "matrix" structure is a compromise between functional and divisional organizations. (See Figure 6-7.) This organizational form

FIGURE 6-6 Typical divisional organization.

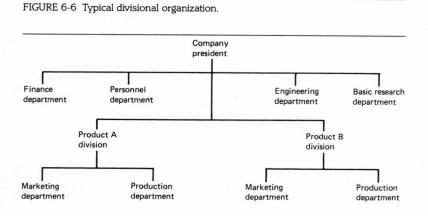

commonly is used for medium-sized and larger companies with closely related, multiple product lines that are often based on similar technologies or distribution channels. Such organizations offer some possibilities for scale or scope economies through the use of shared facilities. Centralized departments—responsible for marketing, production, engineering, and often cost control—report directly to the president; decentralized product managers, or "team leaders," attempt to coordinate these activities for individual product lines.

The advantage of the matrix organizational structure is its potential for joint use of manufacturing, marketing, and technological resources. The disadvantage is that this structural form truly is a compromise between functional and divisional forms. As with all compromises, it is often unsatisfactory. The most unsatisfactory dimension of matrix organizations revolves around the dual allegiances imposed upon functional and technical employees and the uncertain responsibilities divided between functional, technical, and product-team managers.

Matrix organizations always appear attractive because of the expected "expediting value" of product-team managers; they never seem to work as well as expected. We recommend you avoid this form except in the rare instances in which you can achieve absolute clarity of objectives, policies, and programs for each of the units within the matrix and obtain universal agreement upon them.

FIGURE 6-7 Typical matrix organization.

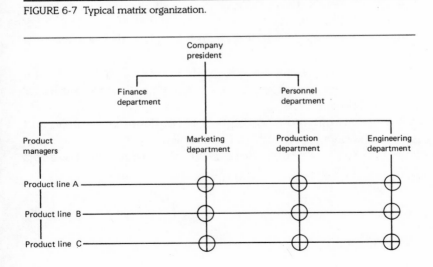

MANAGEMENT SYSTEMS

It is often said that any organizational structure will work if the people involved want to make it work. We do not entirely agree with this statement. Different organizational forms can help or hinder a company depending upon the clarity of the tasks assigned to each position, the ease of communication between positions, and the effectiveness of coordination between people in each of the positions.

Structure does matter. Yet the structure itself is not sufficient to ensure that marketing, production, and financial plans will be carried out. People assigned to each position must know the type of performance expected from them, the standards for performance evaluation, and the rewards for achieving or exceeding these standards. Expectations, evaluations, and rewards are important in the management of smaller companies. They form the basis of management systems for "planning," "control," and "motivation."

Planning develops a competitive strategy (some combination of marketing, production, and financial plans) to react to changes in the business environment and in the specific industry. Planning, next, allocates the resources (financial, physical, technological, and human) to implement the chosen strategy. Finally, it sets the standards for efficient use of those resources.

Control is the complement of planning. It compares actual results of company operations with expected outcomes from the planning process. Control then analyzes the variances (differences between actual results and planned outcomes) and changes the standards if needed.

Motivation, in turn, is the complement of control. It rewards the individual whose performance has brought actual results close to, or above, planned outcomes.

Relationships within the overall process of planning, control, and motivation are shown graphically in Figure 6-8; these systems are interdependent. There are six steps, or stages, in the management systems sequence.

FIGURE 6-8 Relationships among planning, control, and motivational systems.

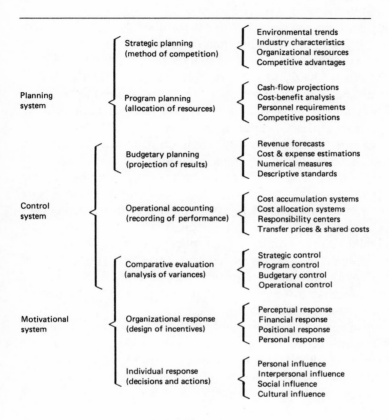

STRATEGIC PLANNING

Strategic planning is the first step in the planning, control, and motivational systems sequence. A popular topic, strategic planning refers to the selection of a long-term method of competition for a firm, and it relates company resources to industry characteristics and business trends. It is hoped that the resulting strategy will provide some form of competitive advantage. Strategic planning chooses a product-market-process position within an industry and then develops integrated marketing, production, financial, and organizational plans for the company that are adapted to that position.

Strategic planning, of course, is what you are doing now to prepare a formation plan for your new venture. If you have followed our recommendations, you began with an analysis of the industry you expect to enter. Next, you selected a product-market-process position within that industry which gives you a reason for success at the start and a competitive advantage over the long run. Then, you developed marketing, production, and financial plans based upon your selected industry position. And now, you are preparing an organizational plan to complete the sequence. You have almost completed your strategic plan.

Why do you have to include strategic planning as an on-going management system in your firm when you have nearly completed your plan? None of the inputs into the strategic planning process—your company's resources; your industry's characteristics; and your nation's economic, political, social, and technological conditions—are static. They continually change. Your strategic plan, consequently, must be continually reviewed and, when necessary, corrected. This continual review and adjustment requires a formal procedure or system to focus attention on industrial and environmental changes and on future opportunities and risks for your firm.

In most organizations, management attention is focused on immediate problems, not on future opportunities and risks. Your strategic planning system should force you to consider the future and prepare for it; numerous examples can be given of small businesses, successful at the start, which failed because company founders failed to consider and prepare for the future.

Formal procedures for strategic planning differ, depending upon the size and diversity of the firm. A small company with a single product or closely related multiple product lines need only establish a regular time for meetings among the president and senior managers and a reporting system on environmental conditions and industry trends. Such a group of executives, tied together by common interests, can examine assumptions about the future, evaluate alternatives for the company, and decide upon changes in the product-market-process position of the firm.

We suggest you and your senior managers meet as a strategic planning committee once every 3 months. Questions to be addressed at these meetings include: "What has changed, creating problems or opportunities for us, since our last meeting? How will these changes in our resources, our industry, or our environment affect us? What alternatives do we have, through modifications to our industry position or to our marketing production, financial, and organizational plans, to respond to these changes? Now, what should we do?"

In many cases, the best response to the last question is, "Nothing different from what we already are doing." There must be a measure of consistency in a company's strategy. You do not want to make a series of small and generally ineffective shifts in your firm's method of competition, but you do want to keep that method current. Strategic planning is often difficult because it must achieve compromises between the opportunities you see and the resources you have, between the need for consistency and the need for change.

PROGRAM PLANNING

Program planning is the second stage in the planning, control, and motivational systems sequence. A "program" can be thought of as the use of company resources—financial, physical, technological, or human—to carry out a portion of company strategy. Introduction of a product line, expansion within a market area, or modernization of a manufacturing plant are three examples of programs. They tend to have a medium time span (2 or 3 years), multiple activities, and extensive assets. Programs are large projects, derived from the strategic plan of the organization. They blend money and talent to reach a competitive position that is defined by strategy.

Program planning specifies the activities and allocates the resources needed to achieve a chosen competitive position. The activities usually are described in general terms, almost on the level of the number of people required to perform functional and technical tasks. (More specific definitions of tasks normally wait until budgetary planning, the next stage in the sequence, during which performance measures are established and achievement targets are negotiated for the assigned personnel.)

Allocation of nonpersonnel resources should not be done on a general or indefinite basis. Small companies and start-up ventures typically suffer from a shortage of resources, especially money, and they have to use the assets they do possess efficiently and effectively. We recommend that you convert the resources needed for each program into financial terms—dollar costs of employing technical people for product design or dollar investments needed for process modernization—and then prepare pro forma cash flows for each program. (A method of estimating future cash flows was described in the previous chapter on financial planning.)

Larger companies usually estimate the cash flows associated with alternative programs and select among them based upon some measure of the expected financial benefits, e.g., the excess of cash receipts over cash disbursements. Financial benefits include after-tax profits and depreciation charges (cash receipts) and investments in working capital, physical facilities, and product-market development (cash disbursements).

A large firm often is able to finance all programs showing an adequate return on capital (the after-tax profits and depreciation from the project divided by the total amount of the investment), but small companies seldom enjoy this luxury. Small companies usually do not have enough cash to finance all programs expected to show a positive return. Program planning in a small company should be done more to anticipate the size and timing of the cash flows—the disbursements and receipts—than to compute the financial benefits. The financial benefits can be assumed if the program can be completed on time, within planned dollar amounts.

We recommend that you and your senior managers meet as a program planning committee once every month. Questions to be addressed at these meetings include: "How are we progressing on our current programs; are we on time and within budget? If not, what changes are needed in the programs, and how will those changes affect our projected cash flow? Do we have enough money to finish our current programs and start others, and if so, which programs should we start next?" The purpose of program planning is to use company resources as efficiently and effectively as possible by forecasting the impact of each program upon the resources of the firm.

BUDGETARY PLANNING

Budgetary planning is the third step in the planning, control, and motivational system sequence. A "budget" is an estimate of revenues, costs, and expenses associated with each program. It details and helps to fine-tune programs. A budget also assigns responsibility for program activities, probably its most important purpose.

A budget is not so much a forecast of results as it is a commitment, by members of a functional or technical department within the organization, to achieve those results. This distinction between a forecast and a commitment is essential to understanding the budgetary planning process—which proceeds from strategy selection to resource allocation to assignments of responsibility. The budget leads members of the various departments to agree to move the company partway toward reaching the proposed competitive position. The overall planning process and differences between its three steps or stages can be summarized according to the time horizon and the conceptual nature of each stage, as shown in Figure 6-9.

The time horizon for each stage represents a typical range, not an absolute requirement, and usually varies by industry. Consumer goods manufacturers often perform strategic planning over 3 to 5 years and program planning over 2 to 3 years. Yet program planning for consumer products with high-style content might be 1 year or less. High-technology companies generally plan on 5-year and 2-year sequences, but both strategic and program planning horizons may be shortened if rapid technological change occurs. Almost all budgetary planning is on

FIGURE 6-9 The three steps or stages of planning.

Planning stage	Time horizon	Conceptual nature of the output of each planning stage
Strategic planning	3-8 years	Selection of a method of competition leading to a competitive advantage for the firm
Program planning	2-5 years	Allocation of resources and assignment of personnel needed to attain the competitive position
Budgetary planning	12 months	Commitment by assigned personnel to achieve goals leading toward the competitive position

a 12-month cycle since the intent is to forecast revenues, costs, and expenses with reasonable accuracy and comparability to the standard fiscal year used in accounting records.

Budgetary planning results in a commitment by members of functional and technical units to use allocated resources to achieve the competitive position envisaged by the company's strategy. Most of the departments within a large firm are responsible for activities related to more than one program; their activities cut across the programs. An overall corporate strategy, therefore, can be viewed as a matrix, with various programs allocating resources and different departments performing activities. (See Figure 6-10.)

Budgetary planning forecasts the revenues and expenses associated with company programs and sets the goals and objectives of functional and technical departments responsible for those programs. Goals and objectives specify expected results in marketing, production, finance, engineering, and so on. They give members of departments a sense of direction and purpose necessary to coordinate their efforts, and they permit evaluation of departmental performance. In short, goals and objectives serve as targets for achievements and standards for control, and they can be expressed as financial, nonfinancial, or nonquantitative performance measures.

FIGURE 6-10 Matrix view of corporate strategy with programs allocating resources and departments performing activities.

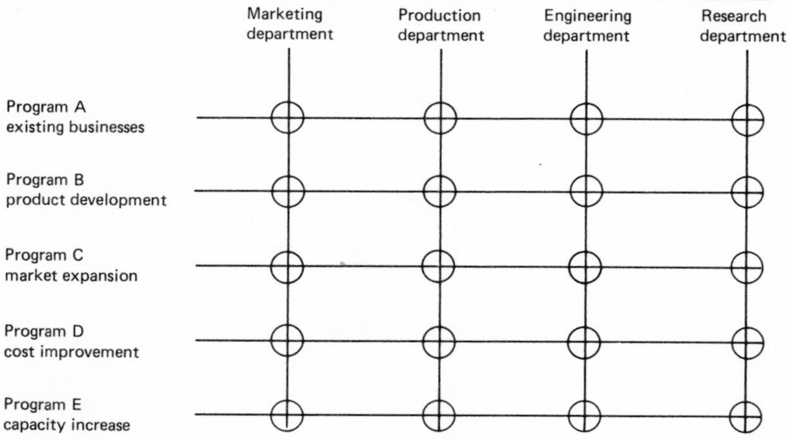

1. **Financial.** Financial performance measures are derived from anticipated revenues, costs, or expenses over a 12-month period. They give the appearance of precision and detail. Yet revenues, costs, and expenses are just summary figures for diverse activities in the functional and technical departments. Financial performance standards do help define areas of responsibility, provide constraints on spending, and compile forecasts of cash flows, but they may not accurately reflect short-term performance. Nonfinancial measures often are needed to supplement them.

2. **Nonfinancial.** Many nonfinancial performance measures are also quantitative. They are derived from "unit" standards such as total output, "ratio" standards such as output per worker, or "percentage" standards such as reject rate or labor utilization rate. Quantitative standards can provide detailed and precise performance measures but only for organizational units in which the output is clearly measurable on a single scale, e.g., line production of homogeneous products. Output from a job shop producing heterogeneous products cannot be measured on a single scale; units per hour or pieces per worker have no meaning when there are wide variations in output type. In these cases input standards offer an alternative means of gauging performance.

   Input standards include such measures as the number of people employed, the number of hours worked, or the number of dollars spent. They rely on the assumption that inputs will be turned into outputs at a steady rate, through a known "input-process-output" relationship. Of course, the problem is that rates may vary for some processes (such as automobile repair) and relationships may not be known for some outputs (such as market research). Consequently, nonquantitative measures often are needed to supplement nonfinancial performance measures.

3. **Nonquantitative.** Nonquantitative performance measures include both subjective estimates of efficiency and surrogate gauges of output. "I think this service organization is working well," is a subjective estimate; it is not a totally satisfactory performance standard. "I think this service organization is working well because there is such a short waiting line," provides an example of a surrogate gauge; it appears more reliable. But think for a few minutes about other possible causes of a short waiting line, beyond prompt attention to customers.

Performance measures for budgetary planning within a small business or start-up venture can be of financial, nonfinancial, or nonquantitative types. These measures also may be of single, multiple, or composite form.

1. **Single.** Single measures are estimates along a single dimension such as profit in dollars, output in units, or input in hours. These measures rely on the assumption that all management activities in a functional or technical department can be summarized on one scale. The corollary, unfortunately, is that all management attention tends to be focused on this scale, often to the exclusion of other important criteria.

2. **Multiple.** Multiple measures use numerous dimensions, such as a combination of the three single measures previously listed. The use of multiple measures avoids the problem of concentrating upon a single factor, but it creates other problems. It may become difficult to reach agreement on more-important versus less-important measures or even on what constitutes "good" performance for a particular organizational unit.

   Suppose, for example, the production department in a new company is producing more output in units than anticipated but at considerably greater cost as measured in input hours. How do you evaluate this? More important—to the overall planning, control, and motivation sequence—how do you reward this? You should anticipate such evaluation and motivation problems during the budgetary planning stage.

3. **Composite.** Composite measures combine multiple dimensions, assigning explicit weighting to each dimension. Single measures from our previous example—profit in dollars, output in units, and input in hours—might all be converted to dollars and then weighted (50 percent on profits, 30 percent on output, and 20 percent on input) to achieve one composite figure. Composite measures theoretically are most satisfactory but tend to be misunderstood by the managers they are intended to help. And composites can become misleading when manipulated to emphasize long- or short-term trends.

Preparing an annual budget probably is the most difficult task in the entire planning, control, and motivation sequence. The budget has to directly follow strategic and program plans without contradicting them.

It must forecast the revenues, costs, and expenses of each program and provide valid performance standards for each organizational unit. Finally, the annual budget has to be understandable and acceptable to managers responsible for keeping programs on time and within budget and for achieving the competitive position envisaged.

We recommend you and your senior managers jointly work out budgetary plans once each year. Participation builds commitment, and commitment to results is what makes the planning process go. One difficulty, however, is that participation often brings arguments rather than agreements. Feelings of frustration may develop as compromises are adopted on standards which one person believes are too easy to achieve and another, too difficult.

Persuade all the managers in your company to approach budgetary planning from the following perspective: "This is how we have decided to compete in this industry (our strategy). These are the resources we are going to use to attain that competitive position (our programs). These, finally, are the results each of us must achieve through our marketing, production, finance, engineering, and other activities in order to use our resources well and quickly attain our competitive position (our budget)."

OPERATIONAL ACCOUNTING

Operational accounting is the fourth stage in the planning, control, and motivational system sequence. It follows budgetary planning, the projection of results, and records these results. Results may be financial, numerical, or qualitative. (The accounting process normally records only financial results; operational accounting is an expanded form, recording both financial and numerical outcomes of managerial activities.)

We obviously cannot explain all the details of accounting here. What we can suggest is that one person on your formation team—this person may be an internal member of your management group or an outside professional—must be a good accountant.

How can you identify a good accountant? It is simple. A good accountant listens carefully as you describe the information you must have to review the progress of programs and performance of departments, and then helps you to accurately and reliably develop that information. A poor accountant, on the other hand, is a person who explains why the information you want cannot be provided. In defense of such a person, there often are technical difficulties imposed by the conventions and regulations of the accounting profession. These conventions and regulations were designed primarily for large firms. For a small company or start-up venture, we do not recommend ignoring or evading them, but we do feel that some degree of flexibility should be observed. In this way, your accountant can provide balance sheets and income statements which accurately reflect the firm's financial position (the primary purpose of financial accounting) and can generate program and budget reports which accurately evaluate company operations.

Program and budget reports, of course, should "tie back" to balance sheets and income statements. In other words, if you add up all the cash flows on the program reports over a given period, you should be able to explain any differences between balance sheets at the beginning and end of that period. And, if you add up all the revenues, costs, and expenses allocated to each of the departments on the annual budget, you should be able to explain the entries in your income statement for the year.

What should you ask your accountant to prepare for your company? There are three fundamental reports needed to manage a small firm. Without them, the firm is likely to manage you. These reports should be prepared monthly, completed by the tenth day of the following month.

1. **A financial report,** including both a balance sheet and an income statement for the company. This financial report probably will have to be prepared by using standard costs for labor, material, and manufacturing overhead, rather than actual charges. (Otherwise, you would have to take inventory each month.) Some of the marketing and administrative expenses also will have to be estimated. (Often, the actual billing for these expenses is not on a monthly basis.) With experience, your standard costs and estimated expenses can become very accurate. We recommend you send a copy of each month's financial report to your bankers and major investors, even if it contains bad news. Bankers and investors like to be kept informed, and they tend to work with companies that do so.

2. **A program report,** showing the cash flows applied to each program and comparing those cash flows to planned amounts. Your accountant should perform variance analysis to explain differences between planned and actual figures. It is also useful to include the total cash flows since the start of each program as compared to total planned amounts. This will help you to determine whether the program is running ahead of or behind the original plan.

3. **A budget report,** indicating the revenues, costs, and expenses allocated to each department and comparing these figures to the budgeted amounts. Again, your accountant should perform variance analysis to help explore reasons for any differences between planned and actual figures. It is often difficult to do variance analysis when working with standard costs and estimated expenses—both of which are needed in monthly financial statements—but much can be done to explain variations between actual and planned amounts, even under such conditions.

COMPARATIVE EVALUATION

Comparative evaluation is the fifth step in the planning, control and motivational systems sequence. Ten days following the end of each month, you and other managers in your firm should receive a financial report, a program report, and a budget report for the preceding month. What should you do with these reports? We strongly recommend you use them to improve performance, not to complain about mistakes.

Information for the improvement of management performance guides the process of comparative evaluation, or "control," as it is more commonly called. Control is effective only when it helps managers and other members of organizational units; it follows management assistance, not repressive standards. Assistance should be provided on three levels, corresponding to the three stages of planning: strategic, program, and budgetary. Control at all three stages compares actual results with expected outcomes and, when necessary, corrects current operations or changes existing plans.

It is tempting to concentrate control efforts on the activities of functional and technical departments. These organizational units generally have financial performance standards which make comparative evaluations easy, short time horizons which make changed results quickly apparent, and low hierarchical positions which make corrective action possible. Such an emphasis upon operating units, however, neglects to evaluate the long-range viability of the selected strategy and the nearer-term completion of funded programs. To improve the overall performance of the firm, control is needed at all three levels—strategic achievement, program efficiency, and budgeted activities.

STRATEGIC CONTROL

Strategic control measures progress in strategy execution. A company's strategic plan defines a method of competition which, over time, should create a competitive advantage. Control evaluates progress toward reaching this improved competitive position. Strategic progress is difficult to evaluate, but some commonly used milestones include comparisons to industry figures on growth rates and market shares, evaluation of company changes in sales revenues and overhead expenses, and competitive comparisons on product designs, brand reputations, distribution methods, and manufacturing facilities. The essential question is: "How well are we doing, as compared to our competitors, in achieving our competitive plan?"

We previously recommended that senior managers of a small company or start-up venture meet once every 3 months to review their selected strategy. This group should assess progress toward achieving the desired competitive position and then consider pertinent changes in organizational resources, industry conditions, and environmental trends. Your purpose should be to continually update and improve the strategy, not to criticize specific managers for past mistakes. Ask yourselves, "How can we do better?" and not, "What have we done wrong?"

PROGRAM CONTROL

Program control measures progress in the execution of programs designed to achieve the long-range competitive position of the selected strategy. Program planning estimates the flow of funds over the life of each program and specifies the activities needed to complete it. Program control compares the estimated usage of funds with actual expenditures and, in particular, compares planned schedules with the actual completions. The essential question is: "How well are we doing on our major programs?"

We previously recommended that senior managers of a small business meet once each month to review progress on various programs. Major variances in resource usage or completion dates should be analyzed and their causes determined. Such discrepancies might prompt changes in programs, activities, or management. Your purpose should be to speed completion, not assign blame. Once again, ask, "How can we do better?" and not, "What has someone done poorly?"

BUDGETARY CONTROL

Budgetary control measures the performance of organizational units responsible for each program's functional and technical activities. Budgetary planning estimates the revenues and expenses associated with each program and sets specific goals and objectives. Budgetary control compares actual outcomes with planned targets for each of the units. The essential question is: "How well are our marketing, production, engineering, and other departments doing?"

We recommend that senior managers meet monthly to review the performance of functional and technical units. The budgetary plan is usually prepared on a 12-month basis, estimating anticipated revenues, costs, and expenses for each month and setting productivity and achievement goals. At the end of each month, variances between planned outcomes and actual results should be analyzed by your accountant. Then, discussion can center on probable causes of variances and proper responses to them. Sometimes it may be important to change your budgetary plans for the balance of the year. Other times, it may seem helpful to alter your organizational activities in various units. Occasionally, you may find it necessary to replace departmental personnel. But think twice before you do the latter. People are rarely the root problem.

We stress the positive side of control—the improvement of performance—rather than the negative side—the assignment of blame. The reason is that most managers of functional and technical units can easily meet budgetary goals over the short run by taking actions destructive to the company over the long run. They can increase sales by offering price discounts. They can reduce expenses by cutting product quality. These are major problems of big business. We do not think they should infect smaller companies, too. Smaller companies should possess the entrepreneurial insight with which to respond intelligently, rather than vindictively, to managerial problems. Use this insight in the management of your company.

ORGANIZATIONAL RESPONSE

Organizational response is the sixth and final stage in the planning, control, and motivational sequence. Generally, it refers to the organizational reaction to management performance as measured by comparative evaluations in the control system. Specifically, it means the design of incentives to reward performance. A planning system becomes a control system when organizational units and individual managers are evaluated according to variances between planned results and actual outcomes at the strategic, program, and budget levels. A control system becomes a motivational system when performance levels, which equal or exceed planned results, are recognized and rewarded.

Recognition is fully as important as reward in companies of all sizes, and recognition is particularly important in small firms and start-up ventures. People like to believe their contributions to the success of an organization are perceived and acknowledged as important by others. One of the organizational benefits of commissions given for sales increases or bonuses awarded for cost reductions is that they provide tangible evidence of this recognition by others. An individual's contribution toward company success becomes acknowledged.

Accepted practices in large corporations, commissions and bonuses should be discouraged in smaller firms. There are two reasons; the first is less important than the second. First, small companies usually suffer from a shortage of resources, and external creditors and investors (banks and venture capital firms) do not like to see money "wasted" on motivational payments. Second, motivational payments should not be needed until a company grows to its nearly final size. People in a smaller firm or start-up venture should be committed to the success of the company, not to personal financial gain at the expense of the company. After success has been clearly established and after the company has grown to a stable size is the time to begin distribution of financial rewards.

We believe two basic concepts of organizational planning deserve stress. The first major concept is that an organization's structure and its management systems should be based upon critical tasks imposed by the strategy of the firm. As strategy changes, critical tasks will change and, consequently, both structure and systems should receive continual attention and updating. The relationships between strategy, tasks, structure, and systems were expressed in a simple chart in Figure 6-1. Refer to it again for emphasis.

The second major concept of organizational planning is that systems or routine procedures for planning, control, and motivation are interrelated. When establishing such procedures, tie together the three levels of planning: strategic planning for reaction to changes, program planning for allocation of resources, and budgetary planning for estimation of revenues, costs, and expenses. Set up regular meetings to evaluate progress and improve performance at all three levels. Always remember, it is the improvement of future performance which will make your company successful, not the assignment of blame for past mistakes.

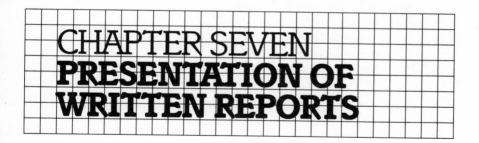

CHAPTER SEVEN
PRESENTATION OF WRITTEN REPORTS

Written reports are required in the management of most business organizations to convey recommendations or instructions and to convince others to implement them. Written reports can be viewed as an end product of the management process; they define organizational problems, identify probable causes, evaluate alternative solutions, and propose specific actions. Ideally, every report should be complete, accurate, and convincing—leading to immediate acceptance.

Many reports prepared for actual situations are not well done. The alternatives considered may not be complete, the analysis performed may not be accurate, or the language and format used may not be convincing.

You are especially prone to such pitfalls in the written presentation of your business plan. It must have something meaningful to say to many different kinds of readers: potential business partners and employees, professional service providers (who may defer fees on the strength of your plan), prospective suppliers (who may offer your new company extended payment terms), and bankers and venture capitalists (who may provide loans for fixed assets and investment funds for working capital). Your business plan ought to be well written. It takes very little extra time to do so, and it does not require natural writing ability. All you need is consideration for, or sensitivity to, the reader.

Recognize that no reader will spend as much time studying a report as the author might wish. Important concepts must be conveyed quickly, clearly, and concisely. In this chapter, we will discuss nine areas of report language and format:

1. Why you should include an executive summary
2. Why you should include a table of contents

3. Suggestions for the report structure
4. Suggestions for the section structure
5. Suggestions for paragraph structure
6. Suggestions for sentence structure
7. Treatment of exhibits and appendices
8. Advantages of comparative charts and matrices
9. Why you should provide definite recommendations

Our discussion is intended to improve the brevity, clarity, and precision of written presentations. Each of our recommendations will be illustrated with good and bad examples from reports on the problems of a small company specializing in the custom remodeling of cars and motorcycles.

WHY AN EXECUTIVE SUMMARY?

Executives in many organizations insist that the major conclusions and recommendations of a report must be clearly stated in a single paragraph on the title page. This "executive summary" serves three purposes:

1. The summary *permits a reader to quickly judge the relevance* of an entire report to his or her interests and responsibilities. In many large firms it is humanly impossible for any one person to read all of the material written by staff, reproduced in large quantities, and distributed to mass audiences.

    Your business plan, similarly, may pass through the hands of many who do not read it completely but judge its worth on the basis of the executive summary. If your summary is deemed of interest, the job of reading the entire document may be assigned to a single staff member in the organization. Later, others may review specific sections of your report.

2. The summary *helps a reader to follow the logic* of your presentation. A degree of suspense may be desirable in fiction, but nearly all business reports are aided by an early statement of major conclusions and recommendations. All the details of reports are easier to understand when the logical outcome is known in advance.

3. The summary *forces the author to reach definite conclusions and recommendations* and to develop essential supporting arguments

for them. It is relatively simple to disguise a lack of content in a lengthy report by reviewing all the alternatives without making recommendations or by investigating all the problems without reaching conclusions. It is more difficult to camouflage such omissions in a brief summary.

A well-prepared summary should list the major conclusions and recommendations of the report—and it should truly summarize. This may appear obvious, but many bad summaries are written as outlines of the content, and others are prepared as explanations of the assignment or as apologies for the result. (The outline should be part of the table of contents, and the explanation of assignment or apology for the result should be placed in a transmittal letter if either is definitely required.)

The purpose of most reports is to define a problem (e.g., a need for equity financing), identify the causes of that problem, and then recommend specific actions for improvement. The summary must condense this content into a single, readily understandable paragraph. A reasonable rule of thumb suggests an executive summary should include three sentences beginning with the phrases: "The major problems are ... "; "The causes of these problems are ... "; and, "Consequently, I recommend that ... " This format may seem too standardized and routine, but it does quickly and understandably convey the conclusions and recommendations of the author.

Consider Examples 1, 2, and 3. Select one which you feel most closely fulfills the three purposes given for an introductory summary.

Example 1

The most immediate problems faced by the Detroit Automotive Corporation are a low level of sales that is much below the break-even point and a negative cash flow that will lead to complete bankruptcy in 6 months. The cause of these problems is a lack of attention to the central issues facing the company, a continual preoccupation with peripheral details, and a continual experimentation with new products and services. I recommend that the company immediately discontinue used car reconditioning (requires mechanical expertise), collision repair (requires price estimating and cost control), and standard customizing (requires production scheduling) and concentrate on the replica manufacture of the MG-TD with a fiberglass body on an American Motors chassis and drive system. Through aggressive advertising and direct sales, this strategy can provide the cash flow needed to rebuild the company.

Example 2

We have examined with care the accounting records, order backlog, and production documents of the Detroit Automotive Corporation, and we have conducted extensive library research and field interviews in the automobile industry. We have reviewed the strengths and weaknesses of the organization, the characteristics and trends of the environment, the values and attitudes toward risk of the management, and the major functional policies and plans to achieve the objectives, and we have prepared the following strategy for your consideration. As part of our analysis, we have prepared pro forma income statements and balance sheets showing the results of this strategy. The resultant report, which we trust you will read with interest and attention, follows. If you have further questions, would you please contact us.

Example 3

This report looks at the functional problems of marketing, production, finance, and engineering; at the organizational problems of unclear assignments and changing directions; and at the strategic problem of the lack of a defined method of competition. Then, environmental factors and organizational resources are evaluated to determine a new strategy for the firm. The value of the new strategy will be directly related to the vigor with which changes in operating and organizational procedures are implemented.

WHY A TABLE OF CONTENTS?

Executives in many organizations require that a one or two page outline be included in the introductory material of written reports. This outline, or "table of contents," also serves three purposes:

1. The table of contents *permits faster reading and clearer comprehension*. Almost all written material is easier to understand (reports are written for understanding, not just for reading) if it is preceded by an outline which graphically displays the logical structure of the content.

   The executive summary, previously described, gives the logical outcome of a report: problem definition, analytical conclusions, and recommended actions. To some extent, the table of contents repeats this information, but it also amplifies and itemizes each section to show the logical structure of the report. The executive summary condenses the opinions of the author; the table of contents explains the thought processes followed in reaching these opinons.

2. The table of contents *permits selective reading with considerable time savings.* Just as every administrator within an organization does not need to read every report, each executive interested in or responsible for a general problem area does not need to read every page of all relevant reports. An outline of conceptual content encourages selective reading.

3. The table of contents *forces the author to consciously design a logical structure,* or sequence of concepts to be presented, before writing a report. Probably the most important element in the presentation of written reports, logical structure also is probably the most neglected. If the logical structure is clear, it is more likely that the content of a report can be understood by the reader. In turn, if the report is understood, it cannot be considered poorly written. Poorly written reports are difficult to read and understand. They fail to show consideration for (or sensitivity to) the reader.

A well-prepared table of contents should list the major concepts of your report, arranged in a logical sequence and displayed on two or more "levels." These levels refer to sections and subsections used to structure and format the content. Each section and subsection should begin with a title heading and a short descriptive sentence. Take ample time to structure the report, to write section and subsection titles, and to compose descriptive sentences.

If the executive summary and the table of contents are clearly and concisely written, the text of the report may be read hurriedly, if at all, and the report's recommendations accepted without hesitance. Often, these introductory materials will convey an immediate understanding of the situation and convince others to act; the text of the report is used only as backup—to describe in detail the analysis performed, the alternatives available, and the specific recommendations made. In a sense, the best-written report is the one that will never be completely read.

Your table of contents should be prepared prior to writing the report's text. You might feel time is not available to write an outline and that to meet some deadline you should start immediately on the text. This is a common feeling and a common failing. It is painfully obvious to a reader when a report has been written without a well-developed logical structure. And usually, not much time can be saved by omitting the structural outline.

At the start, you may think your rate of progress toward completion is slow, but once sections and subsections are blocked out, each with a title and a short descriptive sentence, the balance of the text can be rapidly filled in. Read Example 4, a well-thought-out table of contents, and consider how rapidly the report could be finished by adding descriptive text, exhibits, charts, and matrices.

Example 4

Operating Problems of the Company. Detroit Automotive Corporation has major operating problems in all of the following functional areas:

1. Marketing problems. A consistent marketing plan does not exist in the company; pricing is at a variable multiple of direct costs, and promotional expenditures are spread too widely to be effective.
2. Production problems. An organized productive system does not exist in the company; scheduling is on a personalized basis, and control is lenient at best.
3. Financial problems. The financial position of the company has deteriorated substantially for the past 2 years; current operations are below the break-even point, and a continuation will lead to a negative cash position next March.
4. Personnel problems. The continuing losses and the resultant stresses and disorganized efforts to reach a solution have brought problems of managerial conflict and employee morale.

Strategic Problems of the Company. The executives of the Detroit Automobile Corporation ascribe the operating problems to the recent economic downturn; it is the conclusion of this report that the cause of the problems is not external but primarily internal:

1. Lack of a defined strategy. The company has no defined product-market position; at present the owners are continuing their past efforts at new car customizing and custom parts sales and have added used car reconditioning, collision repairs, sun roof installations, fiberglass fabrications, and classic car reproduction.
2. Lack of definite management. The company has no general manager; our president attends to details such as answering the telephone, talking to parts customers, and purchasing minor supplies. No individual in the management group is attending to the long-term central issues facing the company.

Strategic Alternatives Open to the Company. It would appear that there are five basic alternatives open to the Detroit Automtoive Corporation at this time:

1. Sell the company. This alternative is rejected since neither our president nor the other owners would agree and since the assets of the company have no ready cash value beyond the secured debt.
2. Reduce the size of the company to achieve a lower breakdown. This alterna-

tive is rejected since the investment three years ago in new plant and equipment makes a return to the earlier size and cost structure very difficult.

3. Continue the present diversification strategy of the company. This alternative is rejected since it is anticipated that the diversification strategy will lead to complete bankruptcy unless there is a dramatic increase in the level of economic activity in the Detroit area within the next few months; this increase is not anticipated.

4. Emphasize services for which there is an existing market (used car reconditioning and collision repair) but which require capabilities that the company does not have (price estimating, production scheduling and cost control expertise, and mechanical repair labor). This alternative may be viable.

5. Emphasize services for which a market must be developed (new car customizing and replica manufacture) but which utilizes resources the company now has (style and design engineering, chassis alterations, fiberglass forming, and spray painting). This alternative also may be viable.

Selection of the Strategy for the Company. The strategy of market development (new car customizing and replica manufacture) to increase revenues above the break-even point is recommended, despite the very obvious risk:

1. Major resources of the firm are the style and design engineering and worker competence at chassis alterations, fiberglass forming, and spray painting; the skills needed for production development probably cannot be obtained quickly.

2. Major environmental conditions are the depressed state of the automotive industry and the consequent lack of discretionary income for luxury purchases in the Detroit area. It is felt, however, that a market exists for luxury cars in other sections of the country.

3. Major managerial influences are a high tolerance of risk and a high degree of commitment to customized (individually styled) automobiles.

4. Major time consideration is that a national marketing plan for customized automobiles may be started immediately.

Implementation of the Strategy for the Company. It is suggested that the market development strategy be started immediately with the following functional changes:

1. Marketing plans. Advertising for customized car services and the reproduced classic cars should be started in the major financial papers (*Wall Street Journal, Barrons, Business Week,* etc.).

2. Production plans. Manufacture of ten MG-TD (1947) fiberglass replica cars on an American Motors chassis and drive train and ten Rolls Royce (1932) convertibles on a Oldsmobile chassis and drive train should be started.

3. Financial plans. Complete sale of the used car inventory and reduction of the custom parts inventory should be made to furnish immediate funds for promotion and production. A $50,000 increase in the bank loan will be required.

4. Personnel plans. Wage reduction to all workers, coupled with an explanation of the crisis facing the company, and salary discontinuance to all managers, together with the start of a profit-sharing bonus, should be instituted.

Preparation of a structural outline is the most important step in the presentation of a written report. The following sections discuss language and format suggestions about how to fill in this outline.

SUGGESTIONS FOR THE REPORT STRUCTURE

The structure of your complete report should follow your outline as presented in the table of contents. Fill in the sections and subsections with additional descriptive text and selected supportive data from your analyses. Then utilize typography and headings of different styles to indicate the sequence of sections, subsections, and supporting detail.

1. **Primary sections.** The title of each primary section should be underlined, and the text should be double-spaced, without indentation.
2. **Subsections.** The title of each subsection should be enumerated (1, 2, 3, etc.), and the text should be indented. You might single-space text here for contrast.
3. **Supporting detail.** It's tempting to pack supporting data into the single-spaced text of a subsection, but this makes information difficult to comprehend, and it detracts from the appearance and persuasiveness of the report. Instead, format supporting data beneath each subsection as a chart, graph, table, or matrix.

Example 5, a fragment of an actual report, shows the use of typography and heading styles to separate sections, subsections, and supporting detail. Notice how it makes comprehension quicke and easier for the reader.

Example 5

Strategic Alternatives Open to the Company. Despite the dismal sales performance of the past year and the deteriorating financial position of the firm, there are five basic alternatives that remain open to the Detroit Automotive Corporation. The strategic decision must be made quickly, however, for continued losses will soon block the more attractive options:

1. Sell the company. Our president and the other owners are not in favor of a sale, but a more important reason against this alternative is that it is felt that the company cannot be sold as a going concern under the existing economic conditions in the area, and it is estimated that the liquidation value is below the current liabilities and secured debt:

Account	Book value Sept. 30th	Cash value liquidation	Basis of estimation
Cash	$ (1,442)	$ (1,500)	Additional bank charges for negative balance
Accounts receivable	29,746	22,300	25% discount because of 16 day A/R in cash business
Raw material inventory	13,240	10,600	20% discount on steel, fiberglass, & paint
Sun roof inventory	6,427	3,200	50% discount since difficult to sell
Used car inventory	12,270	11,000	10% discount since sold at auction
Custom parts inventory	28,320	19,800	30% discount since sold to dealers
Advances to employees	4,927	000	100% discount since hard to collect
Building less depreciation	103,909	77,200	25% discount since building is in poor location
Equipment less depreciation	49,793	32,300	35% discount since equipment is special purpose
Total	$247,190	$174,900	Current liabilities & secured debt are $207,700

SUGGESTIONS FOR THE SECTION STRUCTURE

Each section of a business report should primarily deal with one topic (e.g., past problems, current problems, anticipated problems, alternative solutions) and coverage of that topic should be complete. In other words, one topic should not be discussed in two or more sections.

We strongly suggest that each section follow an outlined format, as did the previous example. Write an introductory paragraph (or more) for each section, followed by a series of subsections which amplify and explain the main section's primary topic.

It may seem dull to write, "There are five major environmental trends which will affect the long-term viability of the firm and should be reflected in the competitive posture selected for the company," or, "There are six sequential steps required for the implementation of recommended changes." But such phrases and subsequent listings will quickly and accurately convey an author's meaning to a reader. And, quite frankly, such phrases and listings are simple to write.

1. The content of *each subsection should be limted to one concept* (e.g., short-range financial problems or intermediate financial problems) and generally should be supported with just one graph, chart, table, or matrix.
2. The title of *each subsection should clearly identify the concept* and should be constructed to contrast with other titles. Parallel construction of subsection titles (e.g., pricing problems, promotional problems) provides considerable assistance to the reader.

Examples 6 and 7 have been selected to show the desirability of limiting each section of a report to discussion of a single topic and then structuring discussion on that topic in the form of an introductory paragraph supported by a list of clearly-identified specifics. Each example-writer uncovered two marketing problems during the course of his or her analysis. Which of them more clearly describes these problems to the reader?

Example 6

Promotional literature on Detroit Automotive products might tip the scales in the company's favor. A direct mail campaign should be started to those customers who have visited the dealership but as yet have not made up their minds. Detroit Auto's prices are lower than the industry average, which means that the dealers can sell more strongly the price benefit, which may be important to push dealer selection. Prices are not tied to material or labor cost and vary all over the map. A cost control system should be established quickly by our president or our controller to record costs more accurately. No company can be successful if costs are not known. Material costs should be recorded when delivered. Magazine advertising should be changed since people with money do not read *Hot Rodder* magazine. It is interesting that the decision process for car customizing takes 3 weeks; so promotional literature is best.

Example 7

Operating Problems of the Company. Detroit Automotive Corporation has major operating problems in all of the functional areas; these will be described briefly under the headings of marketing, production, finance, and personnel:

1. Marketing problems in pricing. No firm pricing policy apparently exists; prices as a percentage of direct material and labor vary widely:

Job No.	Material & labor cost ($)	Sales price ($)	Price/cost ratio
23	2138	2086	0.98
46	1777	3400	1.94
11	3788	10900	2.90

2. Marketing problems in promotion. No definite promotional policy apparently exists; the company last year spent more than $28,000 advertising in magazines that probably reached the wrong market segment:

Magazine	Advertising ($)	Comment
Custom Hot Rodder	22,304	Readership of both is assumed to
Dirt Track	6,344	be young, without money for
	28,468	new car customizing.

In Example 7, supporting detail might have been included as part of each paragraph describing a problem. Yet, formatting the supporting evidence, when possible, greatly assists the reader. Spatial relationships make data comparison simple and data significance obvious. If you doubt this, consider Example 8 which contains exactly the same information as before.

Example 8

The direct material and labor cost of job No. 23 was $2138, while the sales price was $2086, for a .98 price/cost ratio. Job No. 46 was sold for $3400, but cost only $1777 which is 1.94 percent. The most profitable job was No. 11, at 2.90 times the direct cost of $3788, which is $10,900. Prices are not set at a constant percentage of fixed and variable costs; improvements in bidding procedures are needed.

SUGGESTIONS FOR PARAGRAPH STRUCTURE

Each paragraph in a business report should focus on a single concept, fact, or point of view. Coverage of that thought or opinion should be complete, i.e., the same concept or fact should not be discussed from the same point of view in two or more paragraphs.

1. **Start with a topic sentence** clearly delineating each paragraph's subject matter. Sentences which follow should support, explain, or elaborate upon that topic.

   Topical sentences are particularly important in business reports because one of the more common forms of speed reading is to scan only the first sentence in each paragraph. It may seem paradoxical for you to prepare a detailed written document for speed reading, but to be effective your report must be read and understood by a wide range of people, people with varying degrees of interest in the information, analysis, and recommendations presented. Topical sentences provide brevity and clarity for this range of readers. They also ensure that each reader (despite the time invested and the reading style employed) will understand the report's major recommendations and reasons for them.

2. **Vary the length of paragraphs,** reflecting the varying need of each topic for support or explanation. Paragraphs in a well-prepared business report tend to be short since much of the supporting data or explanatory detail is formatted or enumerated for rapid comprehension.

   Remember that lengthy paragraphs, with unformatted data or unenumerated detail, often appear disorganized. It becomes difficult for a reader to follow the logical structure created by the author. Detail should support—not obscure—major points, analysis, and recommendations.

3. **Follow an obvious sequence in successive paragraphs** which may be chronological (ordered by time), functional (ordered by activity), or consequential (ordered by importance). Establish this sequence when your outline or table of contents is prepared, and carry it through to the text by using topical sentences which provide natural transitions from one paragraph to the next. If these sequential transitions are omitted, a reader may soon fail to follow the logical argument of the author and, consequently, will lose interest in the content of the report.

   Once again, we strongly suggest you start each section with a topical paragraph describing the content of that section. Begin each subsection with a topical sentence summarizing the content and identifing the logical role of that paragraph within the section.

Example 9 is a paragraph which manages to ignore all our suggestions. Example 10 presents the same information structured in single-subject paragraphs, introduced by topical sentences, supported by variable detail, and organized by natural sequence.

Example 9

Detroit Automotive Corporation was started in 1970 by our president. After a few years work in a gas station in Ypsilanti, the company bought a former DeSoto sales agency and garage in Lincoln Park. Our president may have made a mistake when he moved to Lincoln Park since it is not a good suburb of Detroit. The median income per household in Lincoln Park is only $10,250, and only 15 percent of the families there make over $15,000 per year. The median income per household in Southfield is $19,690, and 68 percent of the families make over $15,000 per year. He also keeps on making a mistake since the shop is not kept organized and clean. He should hire a person to clean the shop, meet the customers, and look after the sale of the custom auto parts. Theft is said to be a problem since the neighborhood has deteriorated. The financial position of the company is so poor (1.4 to 1 debt-equity ratio and .9 to 1 current ratio) that they can not afford to move, but they should at least paint the outside of the building and have better security. They also should rearrange the production, which would not cost much either, to keep the grinding operation out of the showroom. Southfield would be a better location if they can get a bank loan to move there.

Example 10

The company, very simply, is not properly situated, organized, or staffed to successfully market the custom rebuilding of expensive automobiles of higher income clients.

1. The location of the D.A.C. showroom and shop is poor. Lincoln Park is a southwestern suburb in Wayne County, with a low median income per household. The more affluent northern suburbs, such as Southfield, are 20 to 25 miles away in Oakland County, and the only major highway, Route #75, does not come close to the company's neighborhood. The result is that it is difficult to attract customers to the company.
2. The organization of the D.A.C. showroom and shop is poor. The grinding of fiberglass parts, a very noisy and dusty operation, is being done in the showroom part of the building in order to keep the dust from the paint area in the shop. The result is that it is difficult to show customers the products of the company.

3. The staff in the D.A.C. showroom is poor. The grinding of fiberglass parts is the only unskilled operation in the company, yet these are the employees the customer first encounters. They may be described as surly and uncommunicative. The result is that it is difficult to impress customers with the competence of the company.

SUGGESTIONS FOR SENTENCE STRUCTURE

In a book on high-growth ventures, we do not intend to provide detailed instruction on syntax (arrangement of words in phrases and sentences) and grammar (forms of words in phrases and sentences). Syntax and grammar are important. Their rules are complex. These rules probably never will be completely clear to a person who has not studied a foreign language, thoroughly learning the grammatical principles of that language and applying equivalent principles to English composition.

Strict adherence to accepted standards of syntax and grammar should not be your major objective in a business report. Most business readers are oriented toward oral communication, with its characteristic inaccuracies and omissions, and will make similar allowances when reading written reports. You *should* make an effort to correct spelling and to use nouns and pronouns of the proper person and verbs of the proper tense. But first, achieve clarity and stimulate interest. The writer of a business report should develop a "style" (revealed by word choice and sentence structure) which clearly and concisely conveys concepts, facts, and point of view and which holds the reader's attention.

TONE

The tone of sentences does not need to be formal. Some people feel a repressed style ("Yours of the 16th received and contents duly noted . . . ") is required in business. Such archaic phrasing may seem merely dull and boring in a short letter; it will seem absolutely ridiculous in a lengthy report.

A business report's style should reflect the writer's personality. A breezy, informal voice can also be concise and informative. The danger, of course, lies in excess—affecting one extreme or the other. (Good thinking and good writing go hand in hand. If you have trouble expressing yourself, stop and think about it: Why?) Examples 11 and 12 share conceptual content but differ in style.

Example 11

Our president has got to get his act in gear; he has got to decide what he wants to do with his own life before planning where his company is to go.

Example 12

It is essential that our president circumspectly examine his personal ambitions, values, attitudes, and beliefs and then define the overall objectives of the Detroit Automotive Corporation to be consistent with these ambitions, values, attitudes, and beliefs. The relative risk and return of each potential strategy must be examined with care and concern before the strategic decision can be formulated properly.

TERMINOLOGY

The words used in sentences do not need to be specialized. The shared terminology and idiomatic expressions of persons working in the same profession or living in the same social stratum is called "jargon." Jargon also carries a connotation of unintelligibility. To maintain interest and ensure clarity for a range of readers (some of whom may not be acquainted with the specialized terms, and others, so accustomed to them, they seem tedious and dull), you should avoid jargon.

Try using short, simple words, and rely on terms which can be defined in a standard dictionary or technical reference book. Make certain you understand these definitions yourself. Example 13 illustrates the perils of getting in over your head with jargon.

Example 13

Market segmentation studies should be undertaken, to the extent possible under the severe time constraints and adverse financial factors, to determine the parameters of the corporate sales environment and to synthesize the demand analysis.

MEANING

The meaning of sentences should be clear. Clarity is critical in a business report. Nothing is more irritating to readers than a repeated need for studying a single sentence again and again, trying to comprehend the intended meaning. Use sentence structures and phrasing patterns which will promote clarity and help understanding. There are three simple rules. Each sentence should be complete, with an identifiable subject and verb; each sentence should be direct, restricting the number and complexity of modifying terms and phrases; and each sentence should be unified, expressing a single concept, opinion, or recommendation. In Example 14, the writer has neglected all three of these prescriptions.

Example 14

The volume which the large auto-part retailers utilize and its importance to the producers allows them to command wholesale prices which are below its manufacturing cost for all but the most efficient firms whose sales take place in automotive accessories that are highly saturated markets which are themselves susceptible to the economic cycle that now appears to be headed downward.

PHRASING

The phrasing of sentences should be "parallel." Parallelism refers to the use of words and phrases that are similar in structure and form. In a series of nouns, for example, all should be either singular or plural. In a series of verbs, all should be of the same tense. In a series of terms, all should have the same number of modifying adjectives. In a series of phrases, all should have similar verbs and structures.

Parallel structure and form greatly assist in speed reading. They are particularly important in the titles of sections and subsections and in the composition of topical sentences and paragraphs. Example 15 shows how parallelism helps draw a reader through the text of a business report.

Example 15

Marketing plans. Immediate change of marketing plans for the MG-TD (1947 roadster) and the Rolls Royce (1932 convertible) fiberglass replicas is essential for the projected recovery of the firm:

1. Pricing policies. Prices should be set at 2.5 times direct costs; classic auto replicas are a luxury product, and increased prices will help to gain customer acceptance. Prices should be approximately 60 percent of the collector's cost of buying an original vehicle.
2. Distribution policies. Dealers should be established at 25 percent sales commission; replicas are a novel product, and local demonstrations and service will help to overcome customer resistance. Dealers should be reputable garages with an available showroom and interested personnel.
3. Promotional policies. Advertisements should be scheduled at a $25,000 annual rate; replicas are an unknown product, and illustrated ads will help to increase customer contacts. Advertising should be in financial journals, aimed at readers who can afford to buy the cars.

SENTENCE LENGTH

The length of sentences should be varied. One long sentence after another may seem difficult and dull to readers. Variety in sentence length increases reader interest and helps add emphasis. A short sentence such as "Start now." is much more memorable and much more likely to incite the desired response from the reader than the longer one in Example 16.

Example 16

It is critical, in the context of the long-range planning methods proposed for the Detroit Automobile Corporation, that the changes in the functional activities consistent with the newly developed strategy be instituted quickly.

PROBLEMS OF EXHIBITS AND APPENDICES

It is common practice to put quantitative detail—such as comparative financial ratios, expected revenue projections, or investment return calculations—in exhibits attached to the back of the text. These exhibits may be referenced by a short note in the text, e.g., "See Exhibit 5." It is also routine to organize background information on such topics as company history, industry trends, or organizational resources—in appendices attached to the back of the report. One problem plagues both of these methods of including supporting information: exhibits and appendices seldom are read.

You might argue that a conscientious reader should follow instructions given in references or footnotes and should switch from the text to the proper exhibit or appendix and then back to the text. This normally does not happen. The world is not filled with conscientious readers. It is filled with people who want to quickly finish the task at hand so they may go on to others which are more pressing or more interesting.

Executives in business organizations read reports for content. They expect a logical presentation—in an orderly page-by-page sequence. Interruptions in that orderly sequence tend to be ignored. Supportive information, segregated in exhibits and appendices, tends to go unread.

How can knowledge of supporting material be conveyed to the reader? It is simple. Essential information must be summarized within the text; the reader is referred to an exhibit or appendix only for additional detail or explanatory calculations. In Example 17, pro forma financial statements are summarized within the text. Supporting exhibits are referenced. Note that the introductory sentence clearly states the meaning of numerical information.

Example 17

Classic car replica operations for the first year are expected to show a loss, despite severe reductions in existing administrative and engineering expense levels; however, substantial profits should be reached in both year two and year three. (See Exhibit 6 for comparison with current revenues and expenses and supportive details for the forecasts.)

Exhibit 6

	Next Year	Year Two	Year Three
MG-TD (1947) replicas @ $5900 ea.	$ 88,500	$179,000	$267,500
Rolls (1932) replicas @ $14,650 ea.	43,900	102,500	219,700
Custom parts sales @ cost + 25%	20,000	5,000	2,000
Used car sales @ cost − 20%	5,200	—	—
	$157,600	$286,500	$489,200
MG-TD direct costs @ $2200 ea.	$ 33,000	$ 66,000	$ 99,000
Rolls direct costs @ $6400 ea.	19,200	44,800	96,000
Custom parts cost	16,000	4,000	1,500
Used car cost	6,500	—	—
Shop overhead	21,900	35,000	48,000
Gross margin	$ 61,000	$136,700	$247,700

ADVANTAGES OF MATRICES, GRAPHS, AND DIAGRAMS

Solid text can seem dull to readers, even when properly structured in sections, neatly organized in paragraphs, and well-expressed in sentences. Unless the author has an unusually interesting and expressive writing style (most of us do not), it is advantageous to use matrices, graphs, and diagrams. They break up the text and concisely convey large amounts of information.

COMPARATIVE MATRICES

Numerical information in the text of a business report becomes cumbersome. A paragraph containing many dates, ratios, percentages, units, or dollars looks difficult. Most readers skip or skim the material, which often means they will not understand the trends and relationships given.

Example 18 describes the deteriorating financial condition of a company and indicates some of the causes of that deterioration. Few readers would take the time to sort out the meaning of these jumbled figures. Example 19 displays the same quantitative information in a comparative matrix more concisely and convincingly. For obvious trends and relationships, no explanation is needed—beyond an introductory statement which explains major conclusions to be drawn from the figures.

Example 18

The current ratio has gone from 2.4 to 1 three years ago, to 1.8 to 1 two years ago, to 1.3 to 1 last year. Working capital is $29,943 now, but was $79,331 three years ago. Return on sales was 4.3% three years ago, 1.0% two years ago, and −8.6% now. Return on equity was 22.3% three years ago, 6.4% two years ago, and a deficit now. Accounts receivable are now 16, but they were 9 days, and inventory has gone from 44 three years ago to 93 two years ago to 112 last year, while accounts payable have also increased from 12 three years ago to 28 two years ago to 47 last year.

Example 19

Financial problems. The financial position of the company has deteriorated substantially over the past 2 years; this has been caused partially by the operating losses and partially by the continual growth in inventory:

	3 years ago	2 years ago	Last year
Current ratio	2.4	1.8	1.3
Acid-test ratio	1.6	0.9	0.6
Return on sales	4.3%	1.0%	deficit
Return on assets	8.3%	1.4%	deficit
Return on equity	22.3%	6.4%	deficit
Accts. rec. in days	9.0	8.0	16.0
Inventory in days	44.0	93.0	112.0
Accts. pay. in days	12.0	28.0	47.0

Two final suggestions for comparative matrices may seem of minor importance, but they help to quickly convey quantitative information. First, numbers should be carefully selected for inclusion, omitting irrelevant data which may obscure trends and relationships in the matrix. Second, figures should be formatted in orderly rows and columns, making visual comparisons simple and obvious.

INTERPRETIVE GRAPHS

Graphic presentations of quantitative data are less precise than actual numbers displayed in a matrix, but trends and relationships become clear and easy to understand. Use a graph when precision is not critical and when trends and relationships are not obvious.

Charts are particularly useful to show changes in trends and to explain nonlinear relationships. Figure 7-1 illustrates the use of a graph to highlight a linear trend.

FIGURE 7-1 Sample interpretive graph.

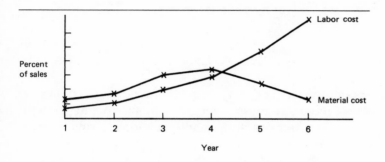

ANALYTICAL DIAGRAMS

A diagram explains relationships, rather than displaying information. A particularly vivid form for business reports is the decision diagram. It can be used to show strategic alternatives and probable consequences of each alternative (or a sequence of decisions and likely outcomes).

Figure 7-2 shows a simple decision diagram. Much more complex forms are possible, examining a wide range of alternatives.

NEED FOR DEFINITE RECOMMENDATIONS

Recommendations are central to a business report. A well-prepared report normally consists of several separate sections on problems,

FIGURE 7-2 Sample decision diagram.

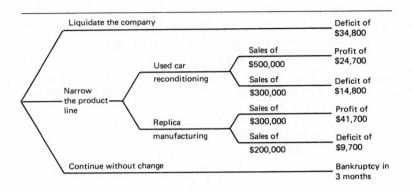

causes of problems, recommendations, and consequences of recommendations.

Many writers attempt to hedge their recommendations, either by discussing each of the alternatives at length without reaching conclusions or by expressing their conclusions in conditional terms (dependent upon other actions or events). It is difficult to hedge on recommendations without being blatantly obvious. You might as well firmly state your recommendations so they can be easily understood and readily followed.

If suggested changes work out poorly, the report author is likely to be blamed anyway, regardless of any qualifications or hesitations. And changes are much more likely to become successful if they are forcefully and convincingly stated. Which of the following recommendations, Example 20 or 21, seems more likely to result in improved performance by the firm?

Example 20

The proposal to build fiberglass copies of classic cars, using purchased frames, motors, and drive train components, seems attractive because of the greatly increased margins if the market develops as expected. If not, then probably the best action would be to recondition used cars and rebuild damaged cars, even though this does not fit the only real skill the company has.

Example 21

I recommend that the Detroit Automotive Corporation concentrate solely on the production and sale of fiberglass classic car replicas. This is the high-risk strategy, but it makes use of existing skills and provides an adequate margin. The probability of success for this strategy may seem low at 70 percent, but it is much higher than for all the other alternatives:

Strategy	Estimated probability of success (%)
Continue company on existing strategy	0
Reduce fixed expenses to level of 3 years ago	20
Concentrate on reconditioning used cars	45
Concentrate on manufacturing replicas	70

Our president can substantially increase the probabilities of success by energetically and enthusiastically implementing the marketing, production, financial, and personnel policies listed in the next section.

We have offered nine ways in which to improve the language and format of written reports and increase brevity, clarity, and interest value. It is often difficult to convert general suggestions into specific words, sentences, and paragraphs. Potential business plan authors should not be discouraged. There is substantial help in reference books available for people who may have limited prior experience in writing, but who also have an assignment to prepare a written document.

RECOMMENDED REFERENCE BOOKS

1. *Rogets' Thesaurus in Dictionary Form,* Berkley Publishing Corporation, New York, 1983. If you have already used the term "environment" twice in a single paragraph and want to find a synonym to avoid using it for a third time, *Roget's* will give you a minimum of twenty choices.
2. *Allen's Synonyms and Antonyms,* Barnes and Noble Books, New York, 1981. This handbook also is alphabetized in dictionary form, making it easy to locate entries. You will find that *Allen's* is slightly

more selective and considerably more precise in providing alternative word choices.

3. *Webster's New World Dictionary,* College Edition, World Publishing Company, Cleveland, 1982. If you are not certain whether a fundamental truth is a "principle" or a "principal," you can look it up in any good dictionary. Dictionaries are useful for the meaning of words, but not for the spelling. They usually do not give the various verb tenses or the noun plurals, areas in which many of us have trouble.

4. *Webster's New World 33,000 Word Book,* World Publishing Company, Cleveland, 1982. The *Word Book* does not give definitions, but it gives spellings in a concise and complete form. If you do not know whether the past tense of the verb "to format" is "formated" or "formatted," you can quickly look it up here.

5. Kierzek, John M. and Walker Gibson, *Handbook for Writing and Revision,* McMillian Publishing Company, New York, 1967. The *Handbook* provides very explicit rules for punctuation and grammar.

6. Bromage, Mary C., *Writing for Business,* 2nd Edition, The University of Michigan Press, Ann Arbor, 1980. Professor Bromage does not offer a reference text, but an engaging description of the various linguistic errors we all commit and helpful suggestions for improvement. This book is to be read and enjoyed, not hurriedly referenced.

APPENDIX A
THE COMPLETED
BUSINESS PLAN

Business Plan for the Michigan Computer Products Company[1]

Executive Summary. The Michigan Computer Products Company manufactures and sells acoustical cabinets for the serial impact printers used in word processing, data processing, and telecommunications. The company has been in existence for 3 years and is currently profitable. At the present time, we have an opportunity to automate our production process, reduce our direct costs, increase our sales volume, and substantially expand our earnings. $353,000 in machinery and equipment and $380,000 in working capital is required. This total of $733,000 can be financed partially by retained earnings, partially by bank debt and equipment leases, and partially by an equity investment of $250,000. The purpose of this report is to solicit proposals for the equity financing.

TABLE OF CONTENTS

1. Office automation is a major trend within the United States, and computer-based printers are part of that trend.

2. Computer-based printers may be divided into line and serial types, and they operate in impact or nonimpact modes.

3. The serial impact printer is the most popular (1983 sales of 420,000 units); it creates the noise problem our product is designed to solve.

---

[1] This is the business plan of an actual company. To provide confidentiality and to avoid releasing proprietary information, the name and location of the firm has been changed and all cost and market information has been altered.

Description of the Industry Product Lines
Page 182

1. The basic problem with serial impact printers in an office environment is their noise; they operate at 65 decibels, which is both tiring and annoying.

2. Our company manufactures acoustical cabinets for serial impact printers; the cabinets reduce the ambient noise level from 65 to 52 decibels.

3. The acoustical cabinets are currently made only in furniture quality models; it is proposed to offer a much less expensive molded plastic unit and an integrated computer workstation.

Description of the Industry Market
Segments   Page 183

1. The market for serial impact printers, and consequently for acoustical printer cabinets, may be divided into five segments:

	1983 printer sales (units)	1983 cabinet sales (units)	Market penetration (%)
Home computer hobbyists	75,600	200	0.2
Small business, internal use	63,000	2,100	3.3
Small business, external use	84,000	5,000	5.9
Medium-sized companies	147,200	35,100	23.8
Large corporations	50,400	20,200	40.1

2. We believe that the penetration is low in most market segments because the proper products (inexpensive plastic cabinet and integrated workstation) are not yet available.

Description of the Industry Production
Alternatives   Page 184

1. Manual fabrication is currently followed by all acoustical cabinet manufacturers; labor cost averages $70.50 per unit.

2. Automated fabrication is possible, using a computer-controlled machining center; labor cost would drop to $43.70 per unit.

3. Plastic fabrication is also possible, using injection molding; labor cost would drop to $4.20 per unit; however the furniture quality appearance would change.

Description of the Economics of the Industry   Page 186

1. The manufacture of acoustical cabinets for serial impact printers is currently characterized by low fixed costs, low break-even, and easy entry.

2. Automation of the production process will change the industry to a high fixed cost, high break-even, and difficult entry pattern, with substantially improved profits.

Description of the Competitive Structure of the Industry   Page 186

1. There are five manufacturers of acoustical cabinets for serial impact printers. All are approximately the same size (800 cabinets per month), and all focus on a limited geographic area because of freight costs.

2. We believe it is possible to dominate this industry by being the first to expand the product line and install automated production equipment.

Company Marketing Plan   Page 188

1. The five market segments have different customer needs, decision processes, and information sources; our marketing plan is adapted to these differences.

2. Pricing will be competitive; with automated processing we can lower the retail price of a typical cabinet from $320 to $244.

3. Distribution will be intensive; we expect to use peripheral equipment dealers, office design firms, office furniture dealers, office supply stores, and personal computer stores, all on a nonexclusive basis.

4. Promotion will be supportive; we expect to advertise regularly in computer oriented, office oriented, and dealer oriented journals.

Company Production Plan   Page 192

1. Automation of the production process will require an investment of $288,100 for machinery and equipment and $38,700 for building modernization.

2. Expansion of the product line (tooling for the molded plastic cabinets) will require an investment of $86,000.

Company Financial Plan   Page 195

1. With automation of the production process, expansion of the product line, and inauguration of the marketing plan, we expect fixed expenses to increase substantially, from $18,480 per month to $53,700 per month.

2. Following the proposed changes, we expect sales during the first year to increase sharply, from a current rate of $1.5 million to a new rate of $4.6 million. This will require an additional $380,000 in working capital but will result in profits after tax of $358,000.

3. Sales in the second year of the expansion and improvement program are projected at $7.6 million, and profits after tax at $730,000. Internal cash flow will provide the additional working capital required for this expansion.

4. The total investment of $732,000 can be financed partially by retained earnings, partially by bank loans and equipment leases, and partially by an equity investment of $250,000.

Company Organizational Plan   Page 198

1. The critical tasks needed to implement the automated production and increased sales have been defined and assigned to specific personnel.

2. Methods to evaluate the performance of those tasks have also been designed and variances from budgeted goals will be reviewed monthly.

Summary of the Business Plan   Page 199

1. Michigan Computer Products Company is a successful and profitable firm. We have developed an explicit business plan to expand our product line, lower our production costs, increase our sales volume, and substantially improve our profitability. This plan requires an equity investment of $250,000. We are willing to discuss both the terms and the conditions of that investment.

Background of the Computer Printer Industry

Office automation is a major trend within the United States. There are differences in the definition of the term, but most people agree that office automation involves the use of data processing, word processing, and direct communications equipment to improve the productivity of both managerial and clerical employees. Individual workstations are provided, with access to a computer through a keyboard terminal and video screen. The computer may be a large mainframe, generally located in the central computer facility, a minicomputer within the department or firm, or a personal unit at the work-station, but the intent is to use the storage and computational capabilities of the computer to improve employee performance.

Printers are needed in an automated office to provide "hard-copy" output, both for internal documents, such as accounting records and production schedules, and for external communications, such as letters and reports. Computer-based printers are made in two basic types, "line" and "serial"; their usage varies depending upon the output speed required.

1. Line printers are for high-speed applications. They print a complete line of type with one motion (operating rates of 400 to 1200 lines per minute are common), and they are normally located in a centralized data processing facility, with a mainframe computer, in which continuous high-volume printing is required. Line printers are generally considered to be too costly, too large, and too complex for decentralized data processing or word processing within an office.

2. Serial printers are for low- and medium-speed applications. They print a single character at a time (operating rates of 10 to 200 characters per second are possible). They generally are used with personal computers or minicomputers, or dedicated word processing systems within an office or laboratory where intermittent, low-volume printing is needed.

Computer-based printers, both the line and serial types, operate with two different modes: "impact" and "nonimpact." The impact mode creates the noise problem which our product is designed to solve.

1. Impact printers operate with a light hammer action. This action may be produced by a multiple striker mechanism, as on a line printer, or with a single striker unit moving across the page, as on a serial printer. The single striker printer can be made with type bars (Telex), a type ball (IBM), a type cylinder (Nippon), a type wheel (Diablo, Qume, etc.), or a dot matrix head (Digital, Epson, Cannon, etc.). The bar, ball, cylinder, and wheel printers are considered to produce "fully formed" or "letter quality" characters; the dot matrix head generates characters formed of minute dots that can, in low density, be difficult to read. Newer versions of the dot matrix printer have greater dot density and approach fully formed characters in legibility.

2. Nonimpact printers use thermal, electrostatic, or ink-jet technologies for both line and serial applications. The thermal and electrostatic methods generate high speeds with minimal mechanical parts (for lower cost and reduced maintenance), but both require special papers which cannot be pre-printed (for payroll checks, purchase orders, company letterhead, etc.). The ink-jet printer can also be used for either line or serial printing; it is a new technology that permits very high speeds and precisely formed characters on regular paper, but it remains a high-cost alternative.

The use of computer-based printers is growing rapidly, as part of the trend towards office automation. Total printer sales are expected to expand from

$2.0 billion in 1983 to $3.6 billion in 1986, at an annual compound rate of 17.8 percent. Sales of serial impact printers, which create the greatest noise problem because of their typical use in an office environment, are expected to increase even more rapidly, at an annual compound rate of 23.8% percent.

	Sales in millions of dollars			
	1983	1984	1985	1986
Line impact printers	1007	1169	1371	1605
Line nonimpact printers	140	165	190	218
Total line printers	1147	1334	1561	1823
Serial impact printers	644	837	1088	1414
Serial nonimpact printers	212	254	309	373
Total serial printers	856	1091	1397	1787
Total line and serial printers	2003	2425	2638	3610

Serial impact printers have become the most popular product type because of their low initial cost and ease of operation. They are available in a range of price and performance levels.

1. $500 or less for a low-speed (ten characters per second) low-density dot matrix printer primarily for home computer usage.

2. $500 to $1000 for a medium-speed (fifty characters per second) low-density dot martrix printer for internal office or report quality use.

3. $1000 to $1500 for a medium-speed (fifty characters per second) high-density dot matrix or striker type printer for external and letter quality use.

4. $1500 to $2500 for a high-speed (100 characters per second) high-density dot matrix or striker type printer, often with graphic capability.

5. $2500 to $4000 for a very high-speed (200 characters per second) striker type printer with proportional spacing, margin justification, and multicolor capabilities.

The market for serial impact printers at the present time is divided into five segments that correspond *roughly* to the five price and performance classifications. Market shares are expressed in terms of units, not dollars.

1. Eight percent for home computer hobbyists who want a means of generating hard-copy printout and are willing to accept the marginal quality of low-density dot matrix printing.

2. Fifteen percent for small business firms and professional offices (doctors and dentists) who use a personal computer or minicomputer for internal accounting and patient billing and also are willing to accept low-density dot matrix printing.

3. Twenty-five percent for small business firms and professional offices (particularly attorneys) who use a personal computer or minicomputer for both internal records and external communications and want letter quality printing.

4. Forty percent for medium-sized business firms and public (government and health care) offices who use decentralized computer systems for word processing, data processing, and some managerial or engineering decision-making.

5. Twelve percent for large business firms who are experimenting with "decision support systems" for managers and engineering personnel and who are also using decentralized data and word processing.

Sales of serial impact printers to large business firms are lower than might normally be expected because of the existance of the "local area network" concept. Most larger companies have very substantial investments in centralized computer systems and integrated databases; the intent of a local area network is to provide access to the database and to utilize excess capacity in the mainframe computer through video terminals at each workstation. All of the terminals within a given area are interconnected (hence the name local area network) so that information can be transmitted between workstations electronically, not in printed form. Consequently, the need for small printers within the local offices is greatly reduced; a single large line printer in the central computing facility can produce most of the documents needed.

Medium-sized and smaller companies, lacking the integrated database and excess machine capacity of larger firms, are working more toward "stand alone systems," with decentralized computers and data storage equipment in each office and with small printers near the workstations for information transfer.

Larger companies may, in the future, also adapt stand alone systems. The local area network concept is attractive because of the use of existing data and equipment and because of the speed of interoffice communication through "electronic mail," but these networks have been slow to develop because of conflicting standards among the major manufacturers (Xerox, Wang, and IBM) and the reluctance of add-on vendors to make major investments in an uncertain market. Now, the decreasing cost of personal computers and the increasing capability of the "superminis" make the decentralized approach to office automation even more attractive. It is unclear, at this time, whether large firms will eventually adopt the stand alone or local area system.

Assuming that the market share of each segment will remain constant over the next 3 years (that is, assuming that large companies do *not* adopt the stand alone system and begin to buy serial impact printers in large numbers), the sales in units of these printers can be expected to be divided as follows:

	Sales in units			
	1983	1984	1985	1986
Home computer hobbyists	75,600	98,100	127,800	166,100
Small business firms, internal	63,000	81,600	106,300	138,200
Small business firms, external	84,000	108,900	141,900	184,500
Medium-sized companies	147,200	190,600	248,200	322,700
Large corporations	50,400	65,200	85,200	110,700
Total sales	420,200	544,400	709,400	922,200

Prior to 1983 390,000 serial impact printers were sold. We estimate that 85 percent of current sales are for new uses, not replacements; consequently, we believe that there will be an installed base of over 2.2 million units by the end of 1986. That represents a large potential market for acoustical covers.

Description of the Product Line

The problem with serial impact printers in an office environment is their noise. Theoretically, an impact printer should be no louder than an electric typewriter because the mechanical action of a type bar or matrix head hitting the paper is similar, but because of the speed at which a printer operates, the noise level is noticeably higher and much more distracting. Typewriters normally run at 45 to 60 decibels and, given adequate sound absorption material in the room to prevent reverberations, the ambient noise level in a busy office tends to average out at about 55 decibels. This sound level does not interfere with ordinary conversations—it is actually considered to be helpful because it provides conversational privacy in an "open" office with low partitions—and it is not thought to be tiring or annoying. Serial impact printers operate at 65 decibels (the decibel scale is logarithmic, not linear, so an increase of 10 points on the scale represents a doubling of the actual sound level). Nearly all conversation stops when a serial impact printer starts, and the noise of the printer is felt to be particularly irritating because it is intermittent, unexpected, and uncontrollable.

Michigan Computer Products Company manufactures acoustical enclosures for serial impact printers. These enclosures, or cabinets, which include an electric fan for cooling, a hinged cover for access, a solid base to reduce vibration, and foam matting to absorb sound, reduce the ambient noise level of an operating printer from 65 to 52 decibels. These acoustical enclosures are, or will be, made in four different models:

1. Molded plastic desktop cabinet, designed to be the least expensive model; our current plan is to add it to the product line next year.

2. Furniture quality desktop cabinet, the most popular model at the present time; as the name implies, it is made to match office furniture in appearance.

3. Furniture quality printer stand, provides storage for paper, ink, and other supplies and permits desk space to be kept for working, not printers.

4. Furniture quality workstation, designed to provide a convenient means of mounting and connecting the keyboard terminal, personal computer, video screen, and serial printer (with enclosure) for a personal workstation.

All of the cabinets, stands, and workstations, except for the molded plastic unit, are made of $\frac{3}{4}$-inch particleboard, laminated on both sides with either a wood grain or smooth finish surface. The six pieces of particleboard (two sides, back, front, top, and baseboard) are rabbetted, or notched, to fit together solidly to control vibration. The interior of each cabinet is covered with 1-inch thick convoluted (waffle surfaced) foam matting to abso⌐ ⌐ sound. The cabinet covers are made of ¼-inch clear acrylic plastic, formed to fit the upper contours of the cabinet and mounted on continuous memory hinges that will maintain the lid in any position (for easy access). Each unit has a cooling fan and an illuminated switch that controls both the fan motor and the printer. (The printer cannot be tuned on without starting the cooling fan, and the illuminated switch serves as a reminder to turn off the unit at the end of the working day.) Three standard colors are available: light oak, dark walnut, or neutral putty (custom colors to match an existing office decor can be provided).

The furniture quality desktop cabinets and printer stands are made in six standard and forty custom sizes to match the full range of serial impact printers. Currently, these printers are manufactured by 30 different firms and are available in 127 different models. The molded plastic desktop unit will be made in two sizes to fit approximately 85 percent of the small (below $700 in purchase price) impact printers and will be available with a standard stand. The workstation will be made with provisions for mounting a keyboard terminal, video screen, personal computer, and printer. The printer will be enclosed in the molded plastic cabinet, set into the bench of the workstation. Computer workstations (also known as office systems or "electronic" furniture) are available now, but none are manufactured with an integral printer cabinet.

Description of the Market Segments

The market for acoustical printer cabinets and stands can be divided into the same segments, basically by size of the company and use of the printer, that were used to subdivide the market for the printers themselves. Industry sales information is not available for printer enclosures, but extrapolating our own sales to include our competitors (four other companies approximately similar in size to Michigan Computer Products plus one or two much smaller firms), we estimate that 62,600 acoustical covers were sold last year, divided between the product types and market segments (greater detail will be found in the section of the report that describes our market planning).

		Sales in units		
	Desktop plastic	Desktop furn. grade	Floor stand furn. grade	Workstation furn. grade
Home computer hobbyists	—	200	—	—
Small business, internal use	—	1,900	200	—
Small business, external use	—	4,300	700	—
Medium-sized companies	—	31,600	3,500	—
Large corporations	—	17,500	2,700	—
Total units	—	55,500	7,100	—

The total sales of printer covers, including both the desktop and floor stand models, last year (1983) were 15 percent of the sales of serial impact printers, or 7 percent of the installed base of those machines at the end of the year. Cover sales were focused in the large corporation (nearly 35 percent of printer sales) and medium-sized company (over 20 percent of printer sales) segments.

Relatively few covers have been sold to the small business and home computer segments. We believe that this is due to the existing designs of the desktop cabinets and floor stands, which are too large and too expensive for small business or home computer use. A customer from these segments might hesitate to spend $320 (average cost of a desktop cover) to enclose a $500 printer, and the need here is for an integrated workstation, not another separate unit. We believe that less expensive and more integrative designs are needed, both for the home computer and small business segments and to expand sales in the medium-sized and large corporation markets. These new designs will require different production methods.

Description of the Production Alternatives

There are basically three alternative production processes that could be used to manufacture acoustical cabinets for serial impact printers. These processes all focus on fabrication of the parts, not upon assembly. The assembly of finished parts into a completed cabinet can be simplified by reducing the number of parts (through molding the base in a single plastic shell rather than joining six pre-cut wooden sections for example) and by facilitating the work (through the use of air-operated clamps and fixtures for another example), but assembly will remain essentially a manual operation. Currently, fabrication of the parts is also a manual operation at all competitors in the industry, but there are two alternative methods, both of which would generate a greater volume at a lower cost, with the added potential of improving quality for the product and safety for the workers. The current manual fabrication and the two alternative methods can be described very briefly (greater detail, of course, will be found in the section of this report on production planning):

1. Manual fabrication. Six particleboard panels must be individually cut to the size and shape specified for each model (on a table saw), the corners have to be rounded to a 2-inch radius (on a belt sander), slots must be cut for the fan opening, paper feed, electrical cord, etc. (on a plunge router), and then forty-three holes must be drilled. A rubber mat has to be cut to size for the baseboard, and the convoluted foam padding cut to size for the sides, back, and front (with a steel edge and hand knife). These are labor intensive operations, subject to worker error and worker injury, that are difficult to facilitate with cutting dies or patterns because of the large number of differ-

ent cabinet models. Labor costs per cabinet for this alternative average $70.50.

2. Automated fabrication. It is possible to cut the six particleboard panels, with corners rounded to the required 2-inch radius and with slots formed for the fan housing, paper feed, etc., doing multiple pieces at one time (up to three layers of particleboard per cycle) on a computer controlled "machining center" for low density (nonferrous) materials. The rubber base and acoustical foam parts may also be cut automatically (up to ten layers per cycle) using a water knife. The system will reduce labor costs per cabinet to $43.70 and also reduce scrap loss.

3. Molded fabrication. It is also possible to form the entire base of the acoustical cabinet (replace the six pieces of particleboard) with an integral fan housing, paper slot, etc., through injection molding. It is proposed to invest only in single cavity dies and to rely on outside vendors for operation of the injection molding machine. This system will reduce labor costs per cabinet to $4.20; however, it will change the furniture quality appearance of the unit.

The operational capacity, labor, material, and variable overhead costs and investment requirements of the three process alternatives are shown below. The investment requirements are limited to essential equipment and tooling only; funds for the construction or modernization of the building are assumed to be equal for all alternatives. Also, as stated previously, the investment for the molded plastic cabinet base is limited to single cavity die set; it is assumed that the injection molding machine will be owned by the outside supplier.

	Capacities & costs		
	Hand fabrication & assembly	Automated fabrication & assembly	Molded fabrication & assembly
Single shift capacity	200/week	1000/week	2500/week
Direct material	$ 62.40/unit	$ 55.40/unit	$41.47/unit
Direct labor[1]	70.50/unit	43.70/unit	4.20/unit
Variable overhead[1]	14.95/unit	11.70/unit	2.70/unit
Total mfg. cost	$161.85/unit	$110.80/unit	$48.37/unit
Investment required	$20,000/line	$228,100/line	$86,000/line

[1]Variable overhead is for power, small tools, and maintenance only; payroll taxes, medical insurance, and employee benefits are included in the labor rate of $11.50 per hour.

Change in the Economics of the Industry

With automation of the production process, which at least some of our competitors must also be considering, the manufacture and sale of acoustical printer cabinets will change from a low fixed cost, low break-even, easy entry industry to a high fixed cost, high break-even and difficult entry pattern. The new pattern will have greater volumes and show greater profits because of the substantial reduction in the variable costs of manufacturing. Detailed pro forma statements are available, of course, in the section of this report on financial planning, but the following very brief summary shows the transformation we expect in the economics of the industry. These are summary statements and do not include, on the positive side, revenues from the new plastic molded cabinets and computer workstation products nor, on the negative side, reductions in price that doubtless will come with greater volume production and increasing competition. The intent is only to illustrate the probable effect of economies of scale and automated production.

	Manual operation (800 units)	Automated operation (4000 units)
Sales revenues per month	$153,600	$768,000
Direct material cost	49,920 (62.40/unit)	221,600 (55.40/unit)
Direct labor cost	56,400 (70.50/unit)	174,800 (43.70/unit)
Variable overhead cost	11,960 (14.95/unit)	46,800 (11.70/unit)
	118,280	443,200
Gross Margin	35,320	324,800
Fixed manufacturing expenses	4,560	19,600
Fixed marketing expenses	10,400	22,400
Fixed administrative expenses	5,800	8,800
Total fixed expenses	20,760	50,800
Pretax profits	14,560	274,000

Current Competitive Structure of the Industry

Currently there are four major producers of acoustical covers for serial impact printers in addition to Michigan Computer Products. All of the firms appear to be approximately equal in size (about 800 covers shipped per month). All tend to focus on a limited geographic area (within 1000 miles of the manufacturing plant) to reduce freight costs since the cabinets are a light but bulky shipment that moves at a high trucking rate. There are differences in product line, price range, and quality appearance, however, and some special features which differentiate the companies:

	HiTek Inc.	Jacobsen Corp.	Colson Company	Printer Products	Michigan Computer
Geographic location	Calif.	Calif.	Minn.	N.J.	Mich.
Product line[1]	Standard	Full	Full	Standard	Full
Price range[2]	$238	$315	$300	$195	$320
Quality level[3]	Good	Good	Okay	Poor	Best
Distribution channels	Direct & dealers	Direct & dealers	Direct & dealers	Direct only	Dealers only
Special features	Extensive advertising	—	—	Ship in kit form	Furniture appearance

[1] Product line is the range of sizes of acoustical cabinets produced by the firm. "Full" indicates that cabinets are available in a variety of sizes to fit any of the 127 different models of serial impact printers; "standard" means that only three to five sizes are available, fitting the most popular of the printers.

[2] Price range is a comparison of the retail price for a cabinet to fit the Epson MX100 printer, one of the most popular models.

[3] Quality level is a subjective judgment based upon the fit and finish of the particleboard base, the thickness of the acoustical foam, and the complete closure of the acrylic cover.

At present, none of the firms in the industry has a competitive advantage nor is a competitive advantage needed as long as the market continues to grow at the current rate. We believe, however, that Michigan Computer Products is best positioned for the future, when competition doubtless will develop as the growth slows and the market matures, by our present policies that emphasize product quality and dealer relationships. The best product line and the largest dealer network will become valuable assets at that time.

Future Competitive Structure of the Industry

An anomaly of the acoustical cover industry is that the market has been left to five small, newly formed firms. Neither printer manufacturers nor furniture manufacturers make or sell acoustical covers. It would be easily possible for a manufacturer of serial impact printers to offer an acoustical cover as an accessory; it would be even more easily possible for a manufacturer of office furniture to add acoustical covers to the product line. So far, neither action has occurred; we expect both to occur at some time in the future.

It is impossible for us, because of our small size, to attempt to establish barriers to entry to protect our market position. We can, however, be prepared. We expect to have an established dealer network, a good product reputation, and the lowest production cost in the industry through economies of scale and learning-curve effects. From that base, we expect to be able to supply acoustical covers to printer manufacturers and be able to compete against furniture manufacturers. The balance of this report describes our marketing, production, financial, and organizational plans to achieve that base.

Marketing Plan

The market for acoustical covers is divided, as we explained in the earlier section of this report on industry background, into five segments marked by the size of the firm and the use of the printer. The needs of customers, the process of buying, and the channels of distribution differ for each of the segments, and our marketing plan is based upon these differences. (A list of typical customers in each segment is in Apendix A;[1] they have agreed to be interviewed by potential investors in our firm.)

1. Large companies. Large firms almost invariably have a centralized data processing department and a corporate data processing staff. Word processing may be decentralized, with stand alone systems within the offices, but these office systems often are tied into the telecommunications and data processing equipment through local area networks. Because of the interconnections, additional office equipment generally has to be approved by representatives from the data processing staff who are responsible for system integration and hardware compatibility.

   Acoustical cabinets are considered to be office equipment, despite the lack of electronic interface, and the responsibility of the data processing staff. These people often are oriented toward technical features of the system, rather than human problems caused by the system. When complaints are made by office personnel about printer noise, the analysts consider acoustical cabinets as if they were peripheral hardware, getting information from printer manufacturers and equipment dealers and making decisions based upon specifications and price rather than appearance and convenience. Orders tend to come in blocks, for 30 to 100 cabinets at a time, and are often sent directly to the cabinet manufacturer, bypassing the dealer. We have refused to accept direct orders, preferring to build up dealer loyalty; this is one reason that our profits have been somewhat lower than those of our competitors, as we have always paid the 40 percent dealer discount.

   We believe, however, that as acoustical cabinets become more common, responsibility for the buying decision will switch from the data processing staff to the person buying office furniture. This person will get information from office designers and furniture dealers, and appearance and price will become the deciding factors. We expect to be represented by furniture dealers and to have our products known by office designers.

---

[1] The appendices have not been included because they were very lengthy and contained proprietary information.

2. Medium-sized companies. A medium-sized firm may have either a single centralized mainframe or a series of decentralized minicomputers, but the technical staff supervising the operation of these machines tend to be less isolated from other employees and more responsive to their needs. Complaints about printer noise go to an office manager, who will generally ask the systems people before buying an acoustical cabinet, but there will be considerably less analysis of competitive models. The office manager will look for information from office furniture dealers and office supply stores, and the final decision will be based more upon appearance and convenience than upon technical specifications and price.

3. Small companies with printers used for external correspondence. These companies buy an expensive printer, use it often, and are aware of the noise problem. They usually rely on software consultants for help with computer equipment rather than on corporate staff, and generally there is no office manager. Instead, an executive who spends considerable time in the office would most likely be the person to make the decision. Sources of information would be the software consultants, office furniture dealers, office supply stores, and (occasionally) personal computer stores. Display models are important, for the small business owner or professional from a law firm or medical clinic often likes to physically inspect office equipment or furniture prior to making a purchase. Appearance, availability, and price are the important factors.

4. Small companies with printers used for internal reports and customer billing only. These tend to have inexpensive printers of the low-density dot matrix type, and small business owners or professionals hesitate to spend $320 to enclose a $495 printer. We believe that this is a primary market for the molded plastic cover and for the computer workstation; many small offices have keyboards, screens, printers, and computers poorly arranged, with inadequate work space. The person making the decision will be the owner of the business or a physician or lawyer from the office, and sources of information will be software consultants and personal computer stores. Product design and price will probably be the deciding issues.

5. Home computer hobbyists. Printers are not used frequently by most hobbyists, and they can easily arrange to be out of the room during printing if the noise is excessively irritating. Printer covers in this market segment may be used more for dust protection than for sound absorption. We also believe that this is a market segment for the computer workstation; and the typical home desk just is not large enough to mount a personal computer and leave room for papers, books, etc. Sources of information will be the personal computer store, and the decision factors will again be product design and price.

In summary, we believe that volume sales of acoustical cabinets for serial impact printers will require representation in multiple distribution channels and promotion through numerous trade journals.

Market segment	Decision personnel	Distribution channels	Promotional means
Large companies at present	Data processing staff	Peripheral equipment dealers	*Datamation* *Computerworld*
Large companies in future	Office furniture buyer	Office designers Office furniture dealers	*Facilities Design* *Office Automation*
Medium-sized companies	Office manager	Office furniture dealers Office supply stores	*Office Automation* *Modern Office* *Office Products Dealer*
Small companies, external use	Executive or professional	Software consulting firms Office supply stores Personal computer stores	*Office Products Dealer* *Datamation* *PC World* *Byte* *Desktop Computing*
Small companies, internal use	Owner or professional	Software consulting firms Personal computer stores	*Datamation* *PC World* *Byte* *Desktop Computing*
Home computer hobbyist	Individual	Personal computer stores	*PC World* *Byte* *Desktop Computing*

Our marketing plan will emphasize median pricing, intensive distribution, and supportive advertising to generate volume sales of acoustical cabinets.

1. Pricing. Our current policy sets the retail price at 2.06 times our direct costs, but this has not generated an adequate margin to cover marketing and administrative expenses and provide a sufficient return. We expect to increase our pricing on the furniture quality cabinets and computer workstations to 2.2 times direct costs. Because of our expected savings in direct costs with the automated equipment, this will still result in a decrease in the retail price to the final customer:

	Direct cost ($)	Wholesale price ($)	Dealer discount (%)	Retail price ($)
Furniture quality now	147.85	192.00	40.0	320.00
Furniture quality then	110.80	146.40	40.0	244.00
Molded plastic cabinets	48.40	64.00	35.0	98.50
Computer workstations	284.00	375.00	40.0	625.00

We believe that it is important to keep the price of the molded plastic cabinet under $100 to attract dealers and generate volume; therefore, the price and discount policies have been changed for this product line.

2. Distribution. We expect to sell the furniture quality cabinets, the molded plastic cabinets, and the computer workstations through peripheral equipment dealers, office design firms, office furniture dealers, office supply stores, personal computer stores, and software consulting companies. Intensive distribution is needed to reach all segments of the market.

    We have prepared a product catalog that is short, colorful, and informative. (See Appendix B.) The different models of the furniture quality cabinets and stands are listed with an explicit classification system to indicate which cabinets will fit which printers. We plan to distribute these catalogs to all dealers within our area.

    Our distribution policy is to sell only through dealers and not directly to the final customer. Our letters to the dealers continually emphasize this policy and its advantages to them. We also plan to contact each dealer, either in person or by telephone, once every 3 months in order to keep our name before them.

3. Promotion. We have prepared an advertising program to reach both dealers and users of our product lines. The ads for the furniture quality cabinets, the molded plastic cabinets, and the computer workstations will have a "family" resemblance, but will stress different features to appeal to the different market segments. Each ad will be $\frac{1}{4}$ page in black and white, with a large illustration and a simple listing of benefits to the customer. The ads will appear in the following groups of journals in a set sequence each quarter:

	Advertising Costs		
	1st month	2nd month	3rd month
Personal Computer World	$1,330	$1,330	$1,330
Byte	1,995	—	1,995
Desktop Computing	—	1,265	—
Computer Dealers	515	515	515
Computer Retail News	865	865	865
Computer Retailer	645	645	645
Datamation	2,080	—	2,080
Computerworld	—	2,012	—
Office Automation	—	2,025	—
Modern Office	1,185	—	1,185
Office Products Dealer	720	720	720
Total	$9,335	$9,377	$9,335

Production Plan

It is possible, as we explained in the earlier section of this report on industry background, to substantially reduce the cost of the acoustical cabinets through automation of the fabrication methods and improvement of the assembly procedures. An automated and improved production process, capable of producing 1000 cabinets per week on a single shift basis, would consist of three separate stages. Each stage has been balanced at the appropriate rate (see Appendix C for operational analysis and standard job times for each stage); minimal in-process inventory will be maintained between the stages.

1. Parts fabrication will be performed on a computer-controlled machine center (see Appendix D for specifications on this machine). The six particleboard panels needed for each cabinet can be cut to finished size, with slots formed for the paper infeed, fan housing, etc., in multiple units (three layers per cycle). The rubber base pad and the acoustical foam mats can be cut to shape on the same machine, using a water knife, also in multiple units (ten layers per cycle). One team of five persons will be assigned to load, operate, and unload the machining center and stack the completed parts by job order number. Members of the team will be responsible for part quality and productivity.

2. Drilling and basic assembly will be performed by a second team of ten persons working in three subgroups with an extra "swing" individual. Each subgroup will have a high-speed radial drill and an adjustable drill jig to accurately position the holes. Each subgroup will also have an assembly station with air-operated clamps to hold the particleboard panels in correct alignment and an air-operated stud driver to fasten the panels. A hot-melt glue system and glue gun will be used to attach the acoustical foam mats and the rubber base pad. Each subgroup will be responsible for basic cabinet quality and productivity.

3. Painting and finish assembly will be done by a third team of five persons. The assembled particleboard cabinet will be protected by a dummy insert (to avoid painting the inside foam) and then sprayed with quick drying paint (for the standard putty color) or with stained varnish (for the walnut and oak grained finishes) in a conveyorized spray booth. Drying will be speeded by an ultraviolet oven on the same conveyor. The person unloading the conveyor will add the company logo and model information with a silkscreen press. A third worker will attach the clear acrylic cover, install the cooling fan, and complete the wiring. The final two workers will inspect and then package the completed units. Each cabinet will be placed in a protective plastic bag and then fitted into a standard carton that will be filled with expanding foam to prevent damage during shipment. Standard-sized cartons will be used to eventually permit automated warehousing. A week's inventory of finished goods will be maintained for prompt shipment of customer orders.

We expect that the assembly of molded plastic cabinets and the computer workstations will be part of the regular production process. This will provide variety for the workers and avoid extra expenditures for additional manufacturing space and equipment.

1. Molded plastic cabinets. The base of this unit has been designed with recessed slots to hold the acoustical foam and with mounting flanges for the cooling fan and electric switch. The cover has been designed with recessed handles and mounting flanges for the hinges. In basic assembly the flanges will be drilled and the acoustical foam mats and rubber base pad will be installed; in final assembly the clear acrylic cover will be added and the fan and control switch attached. No painting is needed, as a neutral putty color is molded into the plastic base. Total labor time, including cleaning, inspection, and packaging, is less than three minutes.

2. Computer workstations. The construction of this unit is identical to that of the furniture quality acoustical cabinet, being made from $\frac{3}{4}$-inch particleboard with laminated surfaces. The parts, of course, are much larger, but they can still be cut on the computer-controlled machining center provided the table and rails of that machine are extended to handle 5×10-foot panels. This extension has been included in our proposed investment. Drilling, basic assembly, painting, and final assembly can be performed on the standard workstations and painting booths, etc., of the regular assembly process.

Staffing of the production process, in addition to the twenty semiskilled workers listed, will require four other people:

1. Shop foreman to supervise the three production stages and to help, when needed, in the setup of the automated machining center. No software competence is needed in this setup; the machine is programmed by design dimensions.

2. Tool grinder to sharpen drills, reamers, and saws and to perform preventive maintenance on the equipment.

3. Shipping clerk to record and store incoming shipments and to dispatch outgoing orders.

4. Janitor to maintain the building and help in the receiving and shipping of orders.

The three production stages and the auxiliary space for inventory storage and shipping/receiving have been designed to fit into our present building, an abandoned auto parts warehouse with a 12-year lease. (See Appendix E for a floor plan of the building and expected placement of the machinery). Some modernization of the building will be required, but the basic structure is sound.

Capital investment for the three new production states, purchase of tooling for the molded plastic cabinets, and modernization of the building totals $356,000. A detailed listing is given in Appendix F, but the major items are shown below:

1. Part fabrication production stage

Computer controlled machining center, delivered	$107,400
Water knife to cut acoustical foam and rubber padding	11,300
Extended machining table to handle 5 × 10-foot panels	4,000
Extended machining rails to handle 5 × 10-foot panels	2,000
Machining center cable hoist	8,700
Machining center jigs and fixtures	4,000
Machining center tooling	8,300
Injection mold for paper slot insert	8,700
Injection mold for fan housing insert	5,700
Total	$160,100

2. Drilling and basic assembly production stage

High-speed radial drills, two more needed	$ 3,600
Adjustable drill fixtures, three needed	3,300
Assembly stations with air clamps, two more needed	2,600
Air stud drivers, two more needed	600
Hot-melt glue system with three glue guns	7,500
Total	$ 17,600

3. Painting and final assembly stage

Paint booth and equipment, with conveyor	$ 8,400
Ultraviolet drying oven, with conveyor	8,200
Fixtures for painting and drying conveyor	1,300
Sprinkler system for paint booth and drying area	5,300
Silkscreen press	3,200
Silkscreens, ten required	700
Assembly station to attach covers, mount fans, etc.	500
Air screwdriver, one more needed	200
Packaging foam machine	1,700
Packaging tape dispenser	100
Total	$ 26,400

4. Miscellaneous equipment for increased production

Repair-parts inventory to avoid machine downtime	$ 14,300
Precision tool grinder	6,300
Air compressor	3,400
Total	$ 24,000

5. Renovation of the building and installation of equipment

Concrete footing for the machining center	$ 2,700
Electrical wiring, 460 volt 3 phase, 500 amps	6,500
Electrical lighting, minimum 100 footcandles	2,800
Compressed air lines for distribution to stages	1,400
Roof-mounted heating units to supplement existing system	7,400
Roof repairs	14,300
Partitions between stages and expanded office	3,600
Total	$ 38,700

6. Purchase of tooling for injection molded cabinets

Single cavity mold for cabinet base	$ 50,000
Single cavity mold for cabinet cover	36,000
Total	$ 86,000

7. Total investment for expanded production $352,800

Financial Plan

The Michigan Computer Products Company was founded in February 1981 with an equity investment of $32,000. Sales did not develop as rapidly as we had expected, and costs were more difficult to control than we had hoped; the result in the first fiscal year (actually 11 months) was a loss of $24,620. Company operations have been profitable since that time, but our continual growth in size (from $343,000 in 1981 to $1,567,000 in 1983) has created credit problems. Detailed financial statements are given in Table 1 at the end of the report; only summary figures are shown here:

	1981	1982	1983
Sales revenues	$343,722	$886,540	$1,567,488
Direct material costs	131,989	325,360	533,217
Direct labor costs	140,863	359,939	591,375
Direct factory	37,121	83,334	127,696
Selling & administrative	58,369	102,980	214,397
Total	368,342	871,609	1,446,667
Profits before taxes	(24,620)	14,931	100,821
Federal & state taxes	—	—	25,678
Profits after taxes	(24,620)	14,931	75,143
Current assets	$27,616	$73,790	$186,032
Machinery & equipment	26,840	22,837	32,405
Leasehold improvements	5,014	17,491	28,223
Prepaid expenses	12,741	10,490	19,706
Total current & fixed assets	72,211	124,608	266,366
Current liabilities	64,831	102,297	168,912
Common stock	32,000	32,000	32,000
Retained earnings	(24,620)	(9,689)	64,454
Total liabilities & equity	72,211	124,608	266,366

Since our poor first year, costs have steadily been reduced and our financial position has gradually been improved. Once again, the full ratio analysis is given in Table 2 at the end of the report and only summary figures are shown here:

	1981	1982	1983
Sales revenues	100.0%	100.0%	100.0%
Direct material costs	38.4%	36.7%	34.0%
Direct labor costs	40.9%	40.6%	37.7%
Direct factory costs	10.8%	9.4%	8.3%
Selling & administrative overhead	17.0%	11.6%	13.6%
Total direct costs and overhead	107.1%	98.3%	93.6%
Profits before taxes	(7.1%)	1.7%	6.4%

After installation of the new production equipment and inauguration of the new marketing plan, we expect our fixed expenses for manufacturing, marketing, and administration to increase substantially. In explanation of our current level of overhead, salaries have been deliberately kept low and the president has served a dual role as the production manager. The following expenses are listed monthly, not quarterly, for easier comparison with typical rates at other companies:

1. Fixed manufacturing expenses per month	Current	Proposed
Production manager	$2,000	$3,000
Tool grinder & assistant foreman	—	2,000
Shipping clerk	900	1,200
Janitor & shipping assistant	—	800
Payroll taxes & employee benefits	640	1,580
Rent for building on fixed lease	1,200	1,200
Heat and light for building	110	240
Depreciation on equipment over 5 years	330	5,880
Insurance on equipment	240	4,270
Taxes on equipment exempt over 5 years	—	—
Total fixed manufacturing expenses	5,420	20,130

2. Fixed marketing expenses per month	Current	Proposed
Marketing manager	$2,000	$3,000
Area dealer manager	—	2,400
Telephone order clerks (2)	900	1,800
Secretaries (2)	750	1,500
Payroll taxes & employee benefits	810	1,510
Telephone expenses	1,470	3,200
Travel expenses	1,560	3,800
Magazine advertising	1,020	9,330
Catalog printing	1,990	3,000
Direct mail	430	3,000
Total fixed marketing expenses	10,930	23,210

3. Fixed administrative expenses	Current	Proposed
President & general manager	—	$3,000
Secretary	—	750
Accounting & bookkeeping	$1,200	1,800
Payroll taxes & employee benefits	240	1,220
Data processing services	—	1,000
Professional services	110	400
Office supplies	30	200
Interest on debt	550	2,000
Total fixed administrative expenses	2,130	10,370

We expect to install the new machinery in a vacant area in our building and then convert the existing production space to finished inventory storage. This will enable us to continue production without interruptions. We also plan to immediately start on the higher level of manufacturing, marketing, and administrative expenses rather than building up to that level by increments. This will permit us to train workers and establish advertising, etc., but it will result in a loss of $16,000 for the first quarter. The first year under the new plan, however, should record an after-tax profit of $358,000, and the second year, $730,000.

	First Year				Second Year
	1st Q.	2nd Q.	3rd Q.	4th Q.	
Furniture quality cabinets					
Unit sales	3,000	5,000	5,000	5,000	20,000
Sales revenues	$439,200	$585,600	$732,000	$732,000	$2,928,000
Direct costs	322,400	443,200	554,000	554,000	2,216,000
Product contribution	106,800	142,400	178,000	178,000	712,000
Molded plastic cabinets					
Unit sales	1,000	2,500	5,000	7,500	30,000
Sales revenues	$64,000	$160,000	$320,000	$480,000	$1,920,000
Direct costs	48,400	121,000	242,000	363,000	1,452,000
Product contribution	15,600	39,000	78,000	117,000	337,000
Computer workstations					
Unit sales	250	500	1,000	1,500	7,500
Sales revenues	$93,800	$187,500	$375,000	$572,500	$2,812,500
Direct costs	71,000	142,000	284,000	426,000	2,130,000
Product contribution	22,800	45,500	91,000	136,500	682,500
Total product contribution	$145,200	$226,900	$347,000	$431,500	$1,731,000
Fixed manufacturing expense	60,400	60,400	60,400	60,400	241,600
Fixed marketing expense	69,600	69,600	69,600	69,600	278,400
Fixed administrative expense	31,200	31,200	31,200	31,200	124,800
Total fixed expense	161,200	161,200	161,200	161,200	644,800

	First Year				Second Year
	1st Q.	2nd Q.	3rd Q.	4th Q.	
Profits before tax	(16,000)	65,700	185,800	270,300	1,086,000
Federal & state taxes	—	10,700	55,700	81,100	356,000
Profits after tax	(16,000)	55,000	130,100	189,200	730,000

We expect to finance the new equipment and the working capital needed for the sales increase through an expanded bank loan (up to 80 percent of the equity), a $100,000 deferred payment note from the manufacturer of the computer-controlled machining center, and an equity investment of $250,000. Pro forma balance sheets are shown in Table 3 at the end of the report.

Organizational Plan

We view the following tasks as critical in the achievement of the dominant (low-cost and high-volume) competitive position in our market area over the coming 2 years:

1. Install and start up the new production equipment. It is essential that this be done on time and within the budgeted amounts.

2. Train the new workers and maintain the present good shop morale and positive group attitudes.

3. Achieve the expected unit output volume despite the need to adjust the production schedule daily to meet customer orders for noninventory units.

4. Maintain an accurate production schedule, reflecting current customer orders for noninventory units and recent order trends by product line and model.

5. Maintain a perpetual inventory record, deducting customer orders as received and adding shop production when completed.

6. Achieve the expected quality standards. Workers at each of the production stages are to be responsible for meeting quality standards.

7. Achieve the expected cost standards. Workers at each of the production stages are also to be responsible for meeting direct labor, material, and overhead cost standards.

8. Purchase material (fiberboard, molded plastic, electrical fans, switches, etc.) from reliable suppliers and insist upon on-time delivery and quality standards.

9. Expand the dealer network to include *all* peripheral equipment dealers, office design firms, office furniture dealers, office supply stores, personal computer stores, and software consulting companies within our sales area.

10. Maintain existing dealers through personal calls on a regular basis to gain market information, ensure sales effort, and resolve possible complaints.

11. Start the advertising campaign to attract dealers and interest customers. The company name is to be recognized nationally at the end of 2 years.

12. Process dealer orders promptly. Incoming orders are to be checked against the perpetual inventory record; items in inventory are to be shipped on the day the order is received. Items not in inventory are to be added to the production schedule, and confirmation of the shipping date is to be sent to the dealer and/or customer.

13. Maintain order records by product line and model type and by geographic area and dealer classification. It is important to recognize trends in dealer order as they occur.

14. Maintain cost records by product line and model type. Direct labor, material, and overhead costs are to be allocated daily.

15. Analyze cost variances by product line and model type. Differences between actual and standard costs are to be reconciled monthly.

16. Prepare monthly statements. Income statements and balance sheets are to be available 5 days after the conclusion of each month.

17. Control current assets. It is important to our financial plans that we stay within the budgeted limits on finished goods inventory and customer accounts receivable.

18. Control manufacturing, marketing, and administrative fixed overhead expenses. Again, it is important to the financial plans that the company stay within the budgeted amounts on overhead spending.

The company is currently organized with a functional structure, and we expect to remain in the format after the expansion of our product line and the addition of the automated equipment. The major positions, task responsibilities, and evaluation procedures will be as follows:

1. Production manager	Install new equipment	On-time start-up
	Train new workers	Worker productivity
	Achieve expected volume	Scheduled vs. actual output
	Purchase raw materials	On-time delivery & standard cost
2. Production workers	Achieve quality standards	Quality defects
	Achieve cost standards	Cost variances
3. Scheduling clerk	Maintain production schedule	Accurate schedule
	Maintain inventory records	Accurate records
4. Shipping clerk	Ship customer orders	On-time shipment

5. Marketing manager	Expand dealer network	Percentage of total dealers
	Start advertising program	Recognition of company name
6. Dealer manager	Maintain existing dealers	Number of active dealers
7. Order clerks	Process customer orders	On-time shipment
8. Accountant	Maintain cost records	Accurate records
	Analyze cost variances	Accurate analysis
	Provide accounting statements	On-time statements
9. President	Control current assets	Actual vs. budgeted
	Control overhead costs	Actual vs. budgeted
	Review employee performance	Actual vs. budgeted
	Plan future expansion	Establish new budgets

At the present time, there are no plans to tie the evaluation of employee performance to the provision of monetary incentives. For the next few years, we believe that the success of the firm is the only motivation needed. After the company is firmly established with a dominant market share, we will establish a commission and bonus plan.

Business Plan Summary

Michigan Computer Products Company is a successful and profitable firm. We have developed an explicit business plan to expand our product line, lower our production costs, increase our sales volume, and substantially improve our profitability. This plan requires an equity investment of $250,000. We are willing to discuss both the terms and the conditions of that investment. Please contact us.

Table 1   Detailed financial statements for Michigan Computer Products Company, 1981 (year of formation) to 1983.

| | 1981 (11 Mo.) | 1982 (Yr.) | 1983 | | | |
			1st Qtr.	2nd Qtr.	3rd Qtr.	4th Qtr.
Cabinets (units)	1,745	4,815	1,744	1,847	2,160	2,413
Sales revenues	$343,722	$886,540	$334,848	$354,624	$414,720	$463,296

	1981 (11 Mo.)	1982 (Yr.)	1983 1st Qtr.	1983 2nd Qtr.	1983 3rd Qtr.	1983 4th Qtr.
Direct material	131,989	325,360	117,196	127,763	137,687	150,571
Direct labor	140,863	359,935	130,255	135,466	155,520	170,116
Direct overhead	37,121	83,334	29,131	30,143	32,348	36,074
Total direct costs	309,973	768,629	276,582	293,372	325,555	356,761
Gross margin	33,749	117,911	58,266	61,252	89,165	106,535
Fixed manufacturing	29,087	41,027	14,047	14,770	14,430	16,261
Fixed marketing	22,140	46,911	30,720	31,754	34,788	32,791
Fixed administrative	7,142	15,042	5,842	5,052	7,533	6,389
Total fixed expenses	58,369	102,980	50,609	51,576	56,771	55,441
Profit before taxes	(24,620)	14,931	7,657	9,676	32,394	51,094
Income taxes	—	—	—	632	9,718	15,328
Profit after taxes	(24,620)	14,931	7,657	9,044	22,676	35,766
Cash	(2,422)	1,132	4,044	3,755	2,882	3,160
Accounts receivable	26,039	59,102	81,851	86,685	115,204	144,136
Inventory—material	3,999	13,556	18,230	24,133	26,007	28,441
Inventory—finished	—	—	2,974	3,940	9,216	10,295
Total current assets	27,616	73,790	107,099	118,533	153,311	186,032
Machinery & equipment	26,840	22,837	26,431	28,711	30,470	32,405
Leasehold improvements	5,014	17,491	21,003	20,618	24,630	28,223
Prepaid expenses	12,741	10,490	14,721	15,044	18,722	19,706
Total fixed assets	44,595	50,818	62,155	64,373	73,822	80,344
Total assets	72,211	124,608	169,254	182,906	226,863	266,366
Accounts payable—material	15,576	54,937	83,814	92,972	81,509	80,489
Accounts payable—other	12,135	15,720	10,742	13,422	12,033	12,460
Loan from bank	—	—	25,000	25,000	55,000	55,000
Loan from machinery	18,620	8,140	7,500	—	—	—
Loan from family	18,500	13,500	12,500	12,500	12,500	12,500
Federal/state taxes	—	—	—	—	4,133	8,463
Total current liabilities	64,831	102,297	139,286	143,894	165,175	168,912
Common stock	32,000	32,000	32,000	32,000	32,000	32,000
Retained earnings	(24,620)	(9,689)	(2,032)	7,012	29,688	65,454
Total equity	7,380	22,311	29,968	39,012	61,688	97,454

Table 2 Financial ratio analysis for Michigan Computer Products Company, 1981 (year of formation) to 1983

	1981 (11 mo.)	1982 (Yr.)	1983			
			1st Qtr.	2nd Qtr.	3rd Qtr.	4th Qtr.
Sales revenues (%)	100.0	100.0	100.0	100.0	100.0	100.0
Direct material (%)	38.4	36.7	35.0	34.9	33.2	32.5
Direct labor (%)	40.9	40.6	38.9	38.2	37.5	36.7
Direct overhead (%)	10.8	9.4	8.7	8.5	7.8	7.7
Total direct costs (%)	90.1	86.7	82.6	81.6	78.5	76.9
Gross margin (%)	9.9	13.3	17.5	18.4	21.5	23.1
Fixed manufacturing (%)	8.5	4.6	4.2	4.2	3.5	3.5
Fixed marketing (%)	6.4	5.3	9.2	8.9	8.4	7.1
Fixed administrative (%)	2.1	1.7	1.7	1.4	1.8	1.4
Total fixed expenses (%)	17.0	11.6	15.1	14.5	13.7	12.0
Profit before taxes (%)	(7.1)	1.7	2.3	3.9	7.8	11.1
Accounts receivable (days)	25	24	22	22	25	28
Inventory—material (days)	10	15	14	17	17	17
Inventory—finished (days)	—	—	—	1	2	2
Accounts payable—material (days)	42	60	64	65	53	48
Accounts payable—other (days)	81	63	57	45	42	38
Current ratio	0.68	0.49	0.77	0.82	0.92	1.10

Table 3   Pro forma balance sheets for Michigan Computer Products Company, 1984 (year of equity investment) and 1985

	1st Qtr.	2nd Qtr.	3rd Qtr.	4th Qtr.	2nd Year
		1st Year			
Cash[1]	$ 5,000	$ 5,000	$ 5,000	$ 5,000	$763,800
Accounts receivable, 20 days	132,500	207,100	316,800	396,000	425,000
Inventory—material, 10 days	21,900	34,200	52,300	65,300	70,100
Inventory—finished, 7 days	35,100	54,900	83,900	104,900	112,600
Total current assets	189,500	296,200	453,000	566,200	1,371,500
Machinery & equipment (net)	346,500	329,200	311,900	294,600	225,400
Leasehold improvement (net)	66,900	65,200	63,500	61,800	55,000
Prepaid expenses	20,000	20,000	20,000	20,000	20,000
Total fixed assets	433,400	414,400	395,400	376,400	300,400
Total assets	623,000	710,600	848,400	942,600	1,671,900
Accounts payable— material, 10 days	21,900	34,200	52,300	65,300	70,100
Accounts payable— other, 30 days	28,000	32,000	36,000	40,000	40,000
Loan from bank	154,600	185,200	150,800	13,400	—
Loan from machinery manufacturer	75,000	50,000	25,000	—	—
Loan from family	12,500	12,500	12,500	12,500	—
Federal/state taxes	—	10,700	55,700	81,100	89,000
Total current liabilities	292,000	324,600	332,300	237,300	236,600
Common stock	32,000	32,000	32,000	32,000	32,000
Convertible debentures	250,000	250,000	250,000	250,000	250,000
Retained earnings	49,000	104,000	234,100	423,300	1,153,300
Total equity	331,000	386,000	516,100	705,300	1,435,300

[1] We expect the large cash balance shown at the end of the second year to be invested in a second manufacturing plant located in the Southwest to expand our market area.

APPENDIX B
DISCOUNTING
PROJECTED EARNINGS

Applicants for venture capital should be aware of a third method of valuing a firm, called "discounting" the projected earnings. This method assumes that a dollar received in the future is worth less than a dollar received today because the money held now can be invested to earn a return that compounds over time. For example, if $2000 is invested now to earn a 40 percent return (typical of the rate expected by many venture capitalists), the investment will grow in an orderly progression. By the end of 5 years it will be worth $10,756.

Invest.	Year 1	Year 2	Year 3	Year 4	Year 5
$2000	$2800	$3920	$5488	$7684	$10756

Adherents to the discounting method argue that the $10,756 realized at the end of the fifth year is worth very much less than that amount today; therefore the $10,756 should be "discounted" back to its "net present value." The discount rate is the reciprocal of the return rate. It may be computed as follows:

$$\text{Discount rate} = \frac{1}{(1 + i)^n}$$

where i = the expected rate of return
n = the number of year

The discount rate for a 40 percent rate of return can be computed for each year as shown below. You will note that the $10,756 from the original investment divided by the discount rate of 5.378 for the fifth year equals $2000, which is considered to be the net present value of the investment.

Invest.	Year 1	Year 2	Year 3	Year 4	Year 5
1.000	1.400	1.960	2.744	3.842	5.378

What does this mean to the person seeking venture capital? Imagine that you have a company currently earning a small profit which can become very successful with an additional investment of $500,000 to expand the product line and improve the production process. Assume that you have developed a business plan and projected your profits and can show that your company will be earning $500,000 per year after taxes at the end of 5 years. Other companies in your industry are valued at 12 times earnings; if your company is treated equally, it should be worth $6 million at the end of 5 years.

Now assume that you approach a venture capital firm and say, "A $500,000 investment now will mean that my company can grow to be worth $6 million in 5 years. Are you interested in sharing this growth?" A partner in the venture capital firm may read your estimates and respond, "Yes, you have an excellent product, a good business plan, accurate projections, and we agree that your company will be worth $6 million in 5 years. But it is not worth $6 million now. That $6 million has to be discounted back to its net present value." The partners will then divide the $6 million by the discount rate for the fifth year of 5.378 and determine a present value of $1.1 million. Their proposed investment of $500,000 is 45.4 percent of that present value, and consequently, they probably will ask for 45.4 percent of the common stock.

INDEX

ABOUT THE AUTHORS

LA RUE HOSMER started a high technology company in New Hampshire in 1956. Since selling the company in 1968, he has earned a doctorate at Harvard and taught small business management, strategic planning, and entrepreneurship. He is currently a full professor at the Graduate School of Business at the University of Michigan and a consultant to numerous small companies in the Midwest.

ROGER GUILES has contributed to several books and authored numerous articles in his 14 years as a professional writer. He has edited various publications of the University of Michigan's Institute of Science and Technology, and directed an annual seminar called "Starting a High Tech Company." Previously, he was bureau chief of McGraw-Hill *World News*, Detroit.